How to Start a Cargo Van and Box Truck Business

Introduction to the Cargo Van and Box Truck Business

Welcome to the exciting world of the cargo van and box truck business! Whether you're an aspiring entrepreneur looking to break into the transportation industry or an existing business owner aiming to diversify your services, this book is designed to guide you through the journey of starting and growing a successful cargo van and box truck business.

The transportation industry is a critical component of the global economy, responsible for the movement of goods and services that keep businesses running and consumers satisfied. Cargo vans and box trucks play a vital role in this industry, offering flexible and reliable solutions for transporting a wide range of items, from small packages to large freight.

Why Start a Cargo Van and Box Truck Business?

1. **High Demand:** With the rise of e-commerce and the continuous need for logistics solutions, there is a growing demand for reliable transportation services. Businesses and individuals alike require efficient and timely delivery services, making this a lucrative market to enter.
2. **Versatility:** Cargo vans and box trucks are versatile vehicles that can be used for various purposes, including delivery services, moving services, and even mobile businesses. This flexibility allows you to cater to

different customer needs and expand your service offerings.
3. **Profit Potential:** With the right business model and effective management, a cargo van and box truck business can be highly profitable. By optimizing your operations and building a strong customer base, you can achieve significant returns on your investment.
4. **Entrepreneurial Freedom:** Starting your own business gives you the freedom to be your own boss and make decisions that shape the future of your company. It offers the opportunity to create a business that aligns with your values and goals.

Key Considerations and Challenges

While the cargo van and box truck business presents many opportunities, it also comes with its own set of challenges. Understanding and preparing for these challenges is crucial for your success:

- **Initial Investment:** Acquiring vehicles, equipment, and necessary licenses requires a substantial initial investment. It's important to plan your finances carefully and explore funding options.
- **Operational Costs:** Managing fuel costs, maintenance, insurance, and other operational expenses can impact your profitability. Implementing efficient management practices is essential to control these costs.

- **Regulatory Compliance:** The transportation industry is subject to various regulations and compliance requirements. Staying informed and ensuring your business adheres to these regulations is critical to avoid penalties and legal issues.
- **Competition:** The market can be competitive, with many established players offering similar services. Differentiating your business through exceptional service, competitive pricing, and innovative solutions will help you stand out.

In this book, we will explore each aspect of starting and running a cargo van and box truck business in detail. From conducting market research and creating a solid business plan to managing operations and scaling your business, you will find practical advice, strategies, and real-life examples to guide you every step of the way.

Let's embark on this journey together and turn your vision of a successful cargo van and box truck business into reality!

Copyright © 2024

All rights reserved. No part of this book may be reproduced in any form or by any electronic or mechanical means, including information storage and retrieval systems, without permission in writing from the publisher, except by a reviewer, who may quote brief passages in a review.

The information contained in this book is for general information purposes only. The information is provided by naciro and while we endeavor to keep the information up to date and correct, we make no representations or warranties of any kind, express or implied, about the completeness, accuracy, reliability, suitability or availability with respect to the book or the information, products, services, or related graphics contained in the book for any purpose. Any reliance you place on such information is therefore strictly at your own risk.

All trademarks and registered trademarks are the property of their respective owners and are used in this book only for identification and explanation.

Permission to use copyrighted material in this book should be obtained from the copyright owner or the publisher.

This book is not intended to provide medical, legal, or financial advice, and the author and publisher specifically disclaim any liability for any loss or damage caused or alleged to be caused directly or indirectly by the information in this book.

Naciro and the publisher of this book do not endorse or recommend any commercial products, processes, or services. The views and opinions of authors expressed in this book do not necessarily state or reflect those of the publisher of this book.

Contents

Chapter 1: Introduction to the Cargo Van and Box Truck Business

- Overview of the industry
- Benefits of starting a cargo van and box truck business
- Key considerations and challenges

Chapter 2: Market Research and Analysis

- Identifying target markets
- Understanding customer needs and preferences
- Analyzing competitors and market trends

Chapter 3: Business Planning

- Developing a business plan
- Setting goals and objectives
- Budgeting and financial planning

Chapter 4: Legal and Regulatory Requirements

- Business registration and licensing
- Insurance requirements
- Compliance with transportation regulations

Chapter 5: Choosing the Right Vehicle

- Types of cargo vans and box trucks
- Factors to consider when purchasing vehicles
- New vs. used vehicles

Chapter 6: Financing Your Business

- Funding options and sources
- Applying for loans and grants
- Managing cash flow

Chapter 7: Setting Up Your Operations

- Establishing a business location
- Acquiring necessary equipment and supplies
- Setting up office and storage space

Chapter 8: Hiring and Training Staff

- Identifying staffing needs
- Recruitment and hiring process
- Training and development programs

Chapter 9: Developing Your Services

- Types of services to offer
- Pricing strategies
- Creating service packages

Chapter 10: Building Your Brand

- Creating a brand identity
- Developing marketing materials
- Establishing an online presence

Chapter 11: Marketing and Promotion

- Marketing strategies and tactics
- Utilizing social media and online advertising

- Networking and partnerships

Chapter 12: Sales Strategies

- Identifying potential clients
- Building a sales pipeline
- Closing deals and maintaining customer relationships

Chapter 13: Managing Finances

- Bookkeeping and accounting
- Managing expenses and revenue
- Financial reporting and analysis

Chapter 14: Implementing Technology

- Essential software and tools
- Utilizing GPS and tracking systems
- Integrating technology into your operations

Chapter 15: Fleet Management

- Maintaining and servicing vehicles
- Scheduling and dispatching
- Managing fuel and other operating costs

Chapter 16: Safety and Compliance

- Ensuring vehicle and driver safety
- Adhering to transportation regulations
- Implementing safety protocols

Chapter 17: Customer Service Excellence

- Providing exceptional customer service
- Handling customer complaints and feedback
- Building long-term customer relationships

Chapter 18: Scaling Your Business

- Expanding your fleet
- Adding new services and markets
- Managing growth and scalability

Chapter 19: Managing Risks

- Identifying potential risks
- Developing a risk management plan
- Insurance and liability considerations

Chapter 20: Sustainability and Environmental Responsibility

- Implementing eco-friendly practices
- Reducing your carbon footprint
- Promoting sustainability in your business

Chapter 21: Networking and Building Relationships

- Joining industry associations and groups
- Building partnerships and alliances
- Attending industry events and conferences

Chapter 22: Leveraging Data and Analytics

- Tracking and analyzing business performance
- Utilizing data to make informed decisions

- Implementing continuous improvement strategies

Chapter 23: Legal and Contractual Considerations

- Drafting and reviewing contracts
- Understanding your legal obligations
- Protecting your business interests

Chapter 24: Handling Logistics and Distribution

- Planning and managing routes
- Coordinating with clients and suppliers
- Ensuring timely deliveries

Chapter 25: Offering Specialty Services

- Exploring niche markets
- Providing specialized transportation services
- Customizing services to meet client needs

Chapter 26: Case Studies and Success Stories

- Real-life examples of successful businesses
- Lessons learned from industry leaders
- Inspiration and insights for your business

Chapter 27: Common Challenges and How to Overcome Them

- Identifying typical obstacles
- Strategies for overcoming challenges
- Learning from failures

Chapter 28: Future Trends in the Cargo Van and Box Truck Industry

- Emerging technologies and innovations
- Industry forecasts and predictions
- Preparing your business for the future

Chapter 29: Building a Legacy

- Creating a long-term vision for your business
- Succession planning
- Leaving a lasting impact

Chapter 30: Conclusion and Next Steps

- Recap of key points
- Actionable steps to get started
- Encouragement and final thoughts

Chapter 1: Introduction to the Cargo Van and Box Truck Business

Welcome to the exciting journey of starting your very own cargo van and box truck business! This chapter will provide you with an overview of the industry, highlight the benefits of entering this market, and outline the key considerations and challenges you may face along the way. Let's dive in!

Overview of the Industry

The cargo van and box truck industry is a crucial segment of the transportation sector, playing a vital role in the logistics and delivery of goods. Whether it's e-commerce deliveries, moving services, or transporting goods between businesses, cargo vans and box trucks are indispensable for ensuring timely and efficient movement of products. The demand for these services has seen significant growth, driven by the rise of online shopping and the need for fast, reliable delivery options.

Cargo vans are versatile, smaller vehicles ideal for urban deliveries, last-mile logistics, and smaller loads. They are often used by courier companies, small businesses, and mobile service providers. Box trucks, on the other hand, are larger and can handle heavier and bulkier items. They are commonly used for moving services, transporting commercial goods, and larger delivery operations.

Benefits of Starting a Cargo Van and Box Truck Business

1. **High Demand:** The increasing reliance on online shopping and e-commerce has led to a surge in demand for delivery services. Consumers and businesses alike need reliable transportation solutions to receive and send goods, making this a lucrative market to enter.
2. **Versatility:** One of the significant advantages of cargo vans and box trucks is their versatility. You can offer a range of services, from small parcel deliveries to large-scale moving services. This flexibility allows you to cater to various customer needs and expand your business offerings over time.
3. **Profit Potential:** With the right strategies, a cargo van and box truck business can be highly profitable. By optimizing your operations, managing costs effectively, and building a loyal customer base, you can achieve substantial returns on your investment.
4. **Entrepreneurial Freedom:** Owning a business gives you the freedom to make decisions, set your schedule, and build something that aligns with your vision. It's an opportunity to create a brand and service that reflects your values and goals.
5. **Scalability:** As your business grows, you can scale up by adding more vehicles, expanding your service areas, and diversifying your offerings. This growth potential

allows you to increase your revenue and build a robust business over time.

Key Considerations and Challenges

While the cargo van and box truck business offers numerous benefits, it's essential to be aware of the key considerations and challenges you may encounter:

1. **Initial Investment:** Starting a cargo van and box truck business requires a significant initial investment. You'll need to purchase or lease vehicles, acquire necessary equipment, and cover licensing and registration fees. It's crucial to create a detailed budget and explore financing options to ensure you have the capital needed to start your business.
2. **Operational Costs:** Managing ongoing expenses such as fuel, maintenance, insurance, and driver wages is vital to maintaining profitability. Implementing efficient management practices, such as regular vehicle maintenance and route optimization, can help control these costs and maximize your margins.
3. **Regulatory Compliance:** The transportation industry is subject to various regulations and compliance requirements. Ensuring your business adheres to local, state, and federal regulations is critical to avoid fines and legal issues. This includes vehicle safety standards, driver qualifications, and operational permits.

4. **Competition:** The cargo van and box truck market can be competitive, with established players offering similar services. To stand out, focus on providing exceptional customer service, competitive pricing, and innovative solutions. Building a strong brand and reputation will help you attract and retain customers.
5. **Technological Integration:** Leveraging technology can enhance your operations and improve efficiency. Investing in GPS tracking, route planning software, and fleet management systems can help streamline your business and provide better service to your customers. Staying updated with technological advancements will keep you competitive in the market.
6. **Customer Expectations:** In today's fast-paced world, customers expect quick, reliable, and hassle-free service. Meeting these expectations requires efficient operations, clear communication, and a customer-centric approach. Developing strong relationships with your clients and understanding their needs will be key to your success.

Getting Started

Now that you have a better understanding of the cargo van and box truck industry, its benefits, and the challenges you may face, you're ready to take the next steps towards starting your business. In the following chapters, we will delve deeper into each aspect of building and growing your cargo van and box truck business. From conducting market research and creating a solid business plan to managing operations and scaling your business, you'll find practical advice, strategies, and real-life examples to guide you every step of the way.

Embarking on this journey requires dedication, hard work, and a clear vision. But with the right knowledge and preparation, you can build a successful and thriving cargo van and box truck business. Let's get started and turn your entrepreneurial dreams into reality!

Chapter 2: Market Research and Analysis

Welcome to the second chapter of your journey towards establishing a successful cargo van and box truck business. Market research and analysis form the backbone of any successful business venture. In this chapter, we will explore the critical steps of identifying target markets, understanding customer needs and preferences, and analyzing competitors and market trends. By the end, you will have a comprehensive understanding of your market landscape, which will enable you to make informed decisions and tailor your services effectively.

Identifying Target Markets

Identifying your target markets is the first crucial step in your market research. It involves defining who your potential customers are and understanding the specific needs that your business can fulfill. Here's how to go about it:

1. **Demographics:** Start by analyzing demographic data such as age, gender, income level, and occupation. For instance, e-commerce businesses might need frequent delivery services, while moving companies might cater to families or young professionals relocating to new areas.
2. **Geographic Location:** Consider the geographic areas you plan to serve. Urban areas might have a higher demand for quick, last-mile delivery services, while suburban or rural areas might require more extensive transportation services for larger items.
3. **Business Segments:** Identify different business segments that could benefit from your services. This could include retailers, manufacturers, wholesalers, construction companies, and event planners. Each segment may have unique transportation needs that you can address.
4. **Consumer Behavior:** Study the purchasing behaviors and preferences of potential customers. For example, businesses with high e-commerce sales may prioritize speed and reliability, while those in the construction industry might focus on the ability to transport heavy, bulky materials.

Understanding what your customers need and prefer is key to providing services that stand out. Here's how you can gain insights into customer needs and preferences:

1. **Surveys and Questionnaires:** Conduct surveys and questionnaires targeting your potential customers. Ask about their current transportation needs, pain points, and what they look for in a transportation service. This direct feedback is invaluable in shaping your service offerings.
2. **Interviews and Focus Groups:** Engage in one-on-one interviews or organize focus groups with representatives from different target segments. These in-depth discussions can provide deeper insights into specific needs and preferences that might not be apparent from surveys alone.
3. **Online Reviews and Feedback:** Analyze online reviews and feedback for existing transportation services. Look for common themes in customer complaints and praises. This can help you identify gaps in the market and opportunities to offer superior service.
4. **Customer Journey Mapping:** Map out the entire customer journey, from initial contact to post-service follow-up. Identify key touchpoints and areas where you can enhance the customer experience. For example, improving the booking process or providing

real-time tracking can significantly boost customer satisfaction.

Analyzing Competitors and Market Trends

A thorough competitor analysis and understanding of market trends will help you position your business strategically. Here's how to conduct an effective competitor and market analysis:

1. **Identify Key Competitors:** Start by identifying your main competitors. This includes both direct competitors (other cargo van and box truck businesses) and indirect competitors (alternative transportation solutions). List their strengths, weaknesses, and market positioning.
2. **SWOT Analysis:** Conduct a SWOT analysis (Strengths, Weaknesses, Opportunities, Threats) for your competitors. This will help you understand where they excel, where they fall short, and potential areas for you to capitalize on or improve.
3. **Market Trends:** Stay updated with the latest market trends and industry reports. This includes advancements in technology, regulatory changes, and shifts in consumer behavior. For instance, the growing emphasis on eco-friendly transportation solutions could be an opportunity to offer green delivery services.

4. **Benchmarking:** Compare your business performance and practices with those of your competitors. Identify industry benchmarks for key performance indicators (KPIs) such as delivery times, customer satisfaction, and cost efficiency. This will help you set realistic goals and measure your progress.
5. **Competitive Positioning:** Use the insights from your competitor analysis to define your unique value proposition. Determine what sets your business apart and how you can offer superior value to your customers. This could be through better pricing, enhanced customer service, or innovative service offerings.

Putting It All Together

Once you have gathered all the information from your market research, it's time to put it all together to form a comprehensive market analysis. Here's how:

1. **Market Segmentation:** Segment your market based on the different target groups you have identified. Define the specific needs and preferences of each segment and tailor your services accordingly.
2. **Customer Profiles:** Create detailed customer profiles for each target segment. These profiles should include demographic information, purchasing behavior, and specific needs. This will help you develop targeted

marketing strategies and personalized service offerings.
3. **Competitive Strategy:** Develop a competitive strategy based on your analysis. Identify your unique selling points and how you can leverage them to attract and retain customers. Consider your pricing strategy, service differentiation, and marketing tactics.
4. **Action Plan:** Create an action plan outlining the steps you need to take to implement your market strategy. This should include timelines, resources required, and key milestones. Regularly review and update your plan based on market feedback and changes in the industry.

Conclusion

Conducting thorough market research and analysis is a critical foundation for your cargo van and box truck business. By identifying your target markets, understanding customer needs and preferences, and analyzing competitors and market trends, you will be well-equipped to make informed decisions and develop strategies that set your business up for success.

Remember, market research is an ongoing process. Continuously seek feedback from your customers, stay updated with industry trends, and refine your strategies to stay competitive. With a solid understanding of your market landscape, you are now ready to move forward and start building a successful cargo van and box truck business. Let's continue this journey together!

Chapter 3: Business Planning

Welcome to Chapter 3 of your journey towards launching a successful cargo van and box truck business. In this chapter, we will delve into the essential aspects of business planning, setting goals and objectives, and budgeting and financial planning. A well-crafted business plan serves as a roadmap for your venture, guiding your decisions and actions as you work towards building a thriving business. Let's explore each of these components in detail.

Developing a Business Plan

A business plan is a comprehensive document that outlines your business goals, strategies, operations, and financial forecasts. It provides a roadmap for how you will start and grow your cargo van and box truck business. Here's what to include in your business plan:

1. **Executive Summary:** This section provides an overview of your business concept, market opportunity, competitive advantage, and financial projections. It should be concise yet compelling, capturing the interest of potential investors and stakeholders.
2. **Business Description:** Describe your business model, including the types of services you will offer, your

target market segments, and the geographic areas you plan to serve. Explain how your business will meet the transportation needs of your customers effectively.

3. **Market Analysis:** Summarize the findings from your market research and analysis. Identify your target markets, customer demographics, and competitive landscape. Highlight any market trends or opportunities that support the viability of your business idea.
4. **Organization and Management:** Outline the structure of your business, including key roles and responsibilities. Discuss your management team's qualifications and experience in the transportation or logistics industry, emphasizing their ability to execute your business plan effectively.
5. **Service Offering:** Provide details about the specific services you will offer, such as same-day delivery, long-distance transportation, or specialized moving services. Explain how these services will differentiate your business from competitors and meet the needs of your target market.
6. **Marketing and Sales Strategy:** Describe how you will attract and acquire customers. Outline your pricing strategy, promotional tactics, and channels for reaching your target audience. Include a sales forecast that outlines your projected revenue based on market demand and pricing strategy.

7. **Operational Plan:** Detail the day-to-day operations of your business, including fleet management, vehicle maintenance, scheduling, and customer service protocols. Discuss any technology or software solutions you plan to implement to streamline operations and enhance efficiency.
8. **Financial Plan:** Provide a detailed financial forecast for your business, including startup costs, operating expenses, revenue projections, and break-even analysis. Outline your funding requirements and how you plan to finance your business, whether through personal savings, loans, or investor funding.

Setting Goals and Objectives

Setting clear and achievable goals is essential for guiding your business towards success. Goals provide direction, motivate your team, and serve as benchmarks for measuring progress. Here's how to set effective goals and objectives:

1. **SMART Goals:** Use the SMART framework (Specific, Measurable, Achievable, Relevant, Time-bound) to define your goals. For example, a SMART goal could be to achieve a certain number of monthly deliveries within the first year of operations.
2. **Short-term vs. Long-term Goals:** Differentiate between short-term goals (achievable within the first year) and long-term goals (achievable over several years). Short-term goals could include acquiring a

specific number of clients, while long-term goals may involve expanding into new geographic markets.
3. **Financial Goals:** Set financial targets, such as achieving profitability within a specified timeframe or maintaining a certain profit margin. Break down your financial goals into quarterly or annual milestones to track your progress over time.
4. **Operational Goals:** Define operational objectives related to fleet management, customer service standards, and efficiency metrics. Consider implementing key performance indicators (KPIs) to monitor and improve operational performance.
5. **Strategic Goals:** Develop strategic goals that align with your overall business strategy. This could include enhancing your brand reputation, expanding service offerings, or establishing strategic partnerships with other businesses.

Budgeting and Financial Planning

Budgeting and financial planning are critical aspects of managing your cargo van and box truck business effectively. Here's how to create a robust financial plan:

1. **Startup Costs:** Estimate the initial investment required to launch your business, including vehicle purchases or leases, equipment, insurance, licensing fees, and marketing expenses. Identify sources of funding, such

as personal savings, loans, or investments from partners or investors.

2. **Operating Expenses:** Forecast your monthly operating expenses, including fuel, vehicle maintenance, insurance premiums, driver wages, and administrative costs. Consider variable costs that may fluctuate based on business demand and seasonal factors.

3. **Revenue Projections:** Develop realistic revenue projections based on market demand, pricing strategy, and sales forecasts. Consider factors such as customer acquisition rates, average transaction sizes, and repeat business opportunities.

4. **Cash Flow Management:** Create a cash flow forecast to track the inflow and outflow of cash in your business. Monitor your cash flow regularly to ensure you have sufficient funds to cover expenses, make loan repayments, and invest in growth opportunities.

5. **Financial Contingency Planning:** Anticipate potential financial challenges or risks, such as unexpected vehicle repairs or fluctuations in fuel prices. Establish contingency plans and reserve funds to mitigate these risks and maintain financial stability.

6. **Financial Metrics:** Monitor key financial metrics, such as gross profit margin, operating expenses as a percentage of revenue, and return on investment (ROI). Use these metrics to evaluate your business performance and make informed financial decisions.

Conclusion

Developing a comprehensive business plan, setting clear goals and objectives, and creating a detailed financial plan are essential steps in laying the foundation for your cargo van and box truck business. By taking the time to plan strategically and anticipate challenges, you can increase your chances of success and effectively manage your business operations.

Remember, your business plan is a dynamic document that should evolve as your business grows and market conditions change. Regularly review and update your plans to reflect new opportunities, challenges, and strategic priorities. With a solid plan in place, you are well-equipped to navigate the complexities of entrepreneurship and build a sustainable and profitable cargo van and box truck business. Let's continue this journey together towards achieving your entrepreneurial goals!

Chapter 4: Legal and Regulatory Requirements

Welcome to Chapter 4 of your journey in establishing your cargo van and box truck business. This chapter will guide you through the essential legal and regulatory requirements you need to fulfill to operate your business legally and responsibly. Navigating these requirements is crucial to ensuring compliance, protecting your business, and building trust with your customers. Let's explore business registration and licensing, insurance requirements, and compliance with transportation regulations in detail.

Business Registration and Licensing

1. **Choosing a Business Structure:** The first step in business registration is choosing a suitable legal structure for your business. Common options include sole proprietorship, partnership, limited liability company (LLC), or corporation. Each structure has different implications for taxes, liability, and operational flexibility.
2. **Registering Your Business:** Once you've chosen a business structure, you'll need to register your business with the appropriate authorities. This typically involves registering your business name, obtaining a federal Employer Identification Number (EIN) from the IRS if applicable, and registering for state and local taxes.
3. **Obtaining Licenses and Permits:** Depending on your location and the nature of your business, you may need specific licenses and permits to operate legally. This could include a commercial driver's license (CDL) for drivers, a business license from your city or county government, and permits for transporting certain types of goods or hazardous materials.
4. **Compliance Check:** Conduct a thorough compliance check to ensure you have obtained all necessary

licenses and permits before starting operations. Failure to comply with regulatory requirements can result in fines, penalties, or legal consequences that could jeopardize your business.

Insurance Requirements

1. **Commercial Auto Insurance:** As a transportation business, obtaining adequate commercial auto insurance is essential. This insurance protects your vehicles, drivers, and cargo in case of accidents, theft, or damage. Coverage should include liability insurance to cover damages to third parties and comprehensive coverage for your vehicles.
2. **Cargo Insurance:** Consider purchasing cargo insurance to protect the goods you transport against loss or damage during transit. Cargo insurance provides financial reimbursement for the value of lost or damaged goods, helping you maintain trust and credibility with your customers.
3. **General Liability Insurance:** General liability insurance protects your business from claims of bodily injury, property damage, or personal injury that may occur during business operations. This coverage can help cover legal fees, settlements, and medical expenses resulting from covered incidents.
4. **Worker's Compensation Insurance:** If you have employees, worker's compensation insurance is

usually required by law. This insurance provides medical benefits and wage replacement to employees who are injured or become ill while performing job-related duties.
5. **Bonding Requirements:** Depending on your location and the nature of your services, you may need to obtain bonding to guarantee performance or fulfill contractual obligations. Bonding provides financial protection to your clients in case you fail to meet agreed-upon terms.

Compliance with Transportation Regulations

1. **Federal Motor Carrier Safety Regulations (FMCSRs):** Familiarize yourself with FMCSRs enforced by the Federal Motor Carrier Safety Administration (FMCSA). These regulations cover various aspects of commercial vehicle operation, including driver qualifications, hours of service, vehicle maintenance, and cargo securement.
2. **State and Local Regulations:** In addition to federal regulations, you must comply with state and local transportation regulations. These regulations may include vehicle registration requirements, weight limits for cargo, and specific rules for transporting hazardous materials or oversized loads.
3. **Driver Qualifications:** Ensure that your drivers meet all qualifications and certifications required by law. This

may include having a valid CDL with the appropriate endorsements, passing medical examinations, and maintaining a clean driving record.
4. **Vehicle Inspections and Maintenance:** Regularly inspect and maintain your vehicles to ensure they meet safety standards and regulatory requirements. Keep detailed records of inspections, maintenance activities, and repairs to demonstrate compliance during audits or inspections.
5. **Environmental Regulations:** Depending on your operations, you may need to comply with environmental regulations related to vehicle emissions and fuel efficiency standards. Implementing eco-friendly practices and using fuel-efficient vehicles can help reduce your environmental impact and compliance costs.

Conclusion

Understanding and complying with legal and regulatory requirements is essential for the success and sustainability of your cargo van and box truck business. By taking proactive steps to register your business, obtain necessary licenses and permits, secure adequate insurance coverage, and comply with transportation regulations, you can operate your business responsibly and minimize legal risks.

Regularly review and update your compliance procedures to stay current with changing regulations and industry standards. Consider consulting with legal and insurance professionals to ensure you have comprehensive coverage and are fully compliant with all applicable laws.

By prioritizing legal compliance and regulatory adherence, you can build a reputable and trustworthy business that meets the needs of your customers while safeguarding your long-term success. Let's continue this journey with a commitment to operating ethically, responsibly, and in accordance with the law.

Chapter 5: Choosing the Right Vehicle

Welcome to Chapter 5 of your journey in establishing your cargo van and box truck business. Selecting the right vehicles is crucial to the success and efficiency of your operations. In this chapter, we will explore the types of cargo vans and box trucks available, factors to consider when purchasing vehicles, and the decision-making process between new and used vehicles. By the end of this chapter, you will be equipped with the knowledge to make informed decisions that align with your business goals and operational needs.

Types of Cargo Vans and Box Trucks

1. **Cargo Vans:**
    - **Standard Cargo Vans:** These are the most common type, suitable for urban deliveries, small loads, and last-mile logistics. They are compact, maneuverable, and fuel-

efficient, making them ideal for navigating city streets and making frequent stops.
- **High-Roof Cargo Vans:** High-roof models offer increased interior height, allowing for easier loading and accommodating larger items. They are popular among businesses that transport bulkier goods or require standing room for workers inside the van.
- **Extended-Length Cargo Vans:** Extended-length vans provide additional cargo space, enabling you to transport more goods or accommodate longer items such as pipes or lumber. They are favored by contractors, tradespeople, and businesses that handle oversized deliveries.

2. **Box Trucks:**
    - **Straight Trucks:** Also known as cube trucks or box trucks, these vehicles feature a separate cargo area attached to the cab. They come in various lengths and capacities, typically ranging from 12 to 26 feet in length. Straight trucks offer ample cargo space and are suitable for medium to large-scale deliveries, moving services, and freight transportation.
    - **Refrigerated Box Trucks:** Refrigerated box trucks are equipped with temperature-controlled cargo compartments, making them ideal for transporting perishable goods such as food, pharmaceuticals, and flowers. They maintain consistent temperature levels to ensure the integrity and freshness of sensitive cargo.

Factors to Consider When Purchasing Vehicles

1. **Payload Capacity:** Evaluate the payload capacity of each vehicle model to ensure it can handle the types

and quantities of goods you plan to transport. Consider factors such as maximum weight capacity, volume of cargo space, and distribution of weight across the vehicle.

2. **Fuel Efficiency:** Opt for vehicles with good fuel efficiency to minimize operating costs and reduce environmental impact. Look for models with fuel-efficient engines, aerodynamic designs, and advanced technology features such as automatic engine shut-off and regenerative braking.

3. **Reliability and Maintenance:** Choose vehicles known for their reliability and durability. Research consumer reviews, manufacturer reputation, and maintenance records to gauge the long-term performance and reliability of each vehicle model. Consider factors such as warranty coverage, service intervals, and availability of replacement parts.

4. **Maneuverability and Accessibility:** Evaluate the maneuverability of each vehicle, especially if you will be navigating tight urban spaces or making frequent stops. Consider features such as turning radius, visibility from the driver's seat, and accessibility of cargo compartments for loading and unloading.

5. **Safety Features:** Prioritize vehicles equipped with advanced safety features to protect your drivers, cargo, and other road users. Look for features such as antilock brakes (ABS), traction control, stability control,

rear-view cameras, blind-spot monitoring, and collision avoidance systems.
6. **Customization Options:** Assess the customization options available for each vehicle model to tailor it to your specific business needs. Consider optional features such as interior shelving, cargo management systems, lift gates, and specialized equipment installations.

New vs. Used Vehicles

1. **New Vehicles:**
    - **Advantages:** New vehicles typically come with manufacturer warranties, updated technology features, and improved fuel efficiency. They offer reliability and peace of mind, requiring less immediate maintenance compared to used vehicles. New vehicles may also qualify for financing incentives and tax deductions.
    - **Considerations:** New vehicles generally come at a higher initial cost, which can impact your startup budget. Depreciation can also reduce the vehicle's resale value over time. Evaluate whether the additional upfront cost aligns with your long-term financial goals and operational needs.
2. **Used Vehicles:**
    - **Advantages:** Used vehicles are generally more affordable upfront, allowing you to acquire multiple vehicles within a limited budget. They may have lower insurance premiums and registration fees compared to new vehicles. Used vehicles also have a proven track

record of performance and reliability based on their previous use.
- **Considerations:** Used vehicles may have higher maintenance requirements and repair costs compared to new vehicles. It's essential to conduct a thorough inspection and review maintenance records to assess the vehicle's condition and potential longevity. Consider purchasing from reputable dealerships or private sellers to ensure transparency and reliability.

Conclusion

Choosing the right vehicles for your cargo van and box truck business is a critical decision that impacts your operational efficiency, customer satisfaction, and overall profitability. By understanding the types of vehicles available, evaluating key factors such as payload capacity and fuel efficiency, and weighing the pros and cons of new versus used vehicles, you can make informed decisions that support your business objectives.

Take the time to research and compare vehicle models, consult with industry experts, and consider your long-term business strategy when making purchasing decisions. Investing in reliable, well-maintained vehicles that meet your specific operational needs will set the foundation for a successful and sustainable cargo van and box truck business. Let's continue this journey with confidence as you build and expand your fleet to deliver exceptional service to your customers.

Chapter 6: Financing Your Business

Welcome to Chapter 6 of your journey in establishing your cargo van and box truck business. Financing your business is a crucial step towards turning your entrepreneurial vision into reality. In this chapter, we will explore various funding options and sources, discuss the process of applying for loans and grants, and provide insights on managing cash flow effectively. By understanding these aspects of business finance, you can make informed decisions to secure the necessary capital and ensure the financial health of your business.

Funding Options and Sources

1. **Personal Savings:** Using personal savings is a common way to fund a startup business. It allows you to retain full ownership and control over your business without taking on debt or external investors. Evaluate your savings and consider how much you are willing to invest in your cargo van and box truck business.
2. **Family and Friends:** Borrowing from family or friends can provide initial capital with flexible terms and potentially lower interest rates compared to traditional lenders. Clearly communicate expectations and terms to avoid misunderstandings and maintain healthy relationships.
3. **Small Business Loans:** Small business loans are a popular financing option for entrepreneurs. These

loans are offered by banks, credit unions, and online lenders and can be used to cover startup costs, purchase equipment, or fund operational expenses. Research different lenders, compare interest rates and terms, and prepare a solid business plan to increase your chances of approval.

4. **Business Credit Cards:** Business credit cards offer a convenient way to finance small purchases and manage cash flow. They often come with rewards programs and expense tracking tools. Use business credit cards responsibly to build your business credit profile and manage expenses effectively.
5. **Crowdfunding:** Crowdfunding platforms allow you to raise capital from a large number of individuals who contribute small amounts of money to support your business idea. Create a compelling campaign, set fundraising goals, and offer rewards or incentives to attract backers. Platforms like Kickstarter and Indiegogo are popular options for crowdfunding campaigns.
6. **Angel Investors and Venture Capital:** Angel investors and venture capital firms provide funding in exchange for equity or ownership stake in your business. They typically invest in high-growth startups with potential for substantial returns. Prepare a comprehensive business plan, financial projections, and a compelling pitch to attract investors.

7. **Government Grants and Programs:** Research government grants and programs that provide funding to small businesses, particularly in the transportation and logistics sector. These grants may have specific eligibility criteria and application requirements. Visit government websites or consult with a business advisor to explore available opportunities.

Applying for Loans and Grants

1. **Prepare a Business Plan:** A well-crafted business plan is essential when applying for loans or grants. Outline your business concept, market analysis, competitive advantage, and financial projections. Clearly articulate how the funding will be used and the expected impact on your business growth.
2. **Research Lenders and Grant Programs:** Research different lenders, grant programs, and eligibility criteria. Identify lenders or programs that specialize in small business financing or support industries related to transportation and logistics. Tailor your applications to match specific requirements and guidelines.
3. **Gather Documentation:** Gather necessary documentation such as financial statements, tax returns, business licenses, and personal identification. Lenders and grant programs may require proof of income, credit history, and collateral for secured loans.

Organize your documents to streamline the application process.
4. **Submit Applications:** Submit loan applications or grant proposals according to the instructions provided by each lender or program. Pay attention to deadlines and ensure your application is complete and accurate. Include supporting documents and any additional information requested to strengthen your case.
5. **Follow Up:** After submitting your applications, follow up with lenders or grant administrators to track the progress of your application. Be prepared to respond to any questions or requests for additional information promptly. Maintain open communication to demonstrate your commitment and professionalism.

Managing Cash Flow

1. **Create a Cash Flow Forecast:** Develop a cash flow forecast to track the inflow and outflow of cash in your business on a monthly or quarterly basis. Anticipate revenue from deliveries, customer payments, and other sources, as well as expenses such as vehicle maintenance, fuel, insurance premiums, and operational costs.
2. **Monitor Accounts Receivable and Payable:** Keep track of accounts receivable (money owed to your business) and accounts payable (money your business owes to suppliers and creditors). Establish clear payment terms

with customers and suppliers to maintain a healthy cash flow cycle.

3. **Control Expenses:** Monitor and control business expenses to minimize unnecessary spending and improve cash flow. Negotiate favorable terms with suppliers, explore cost-saving opportunities, and review recurring expenses regularly.
4. **Build a Cash Reserve:** Build a cash reserve or emergency fund to cover unexpected expenses, fluctuations in revenue, or temporary cash flow gaps. Aim to maintain a buffer that can sustain your business operations during challenging times without relying solely on external financing.
5. **Use Financing Wisely:** Use borrowed funds and credit responsibly to support business growth and expansion. Avoid overleveraging your business and prioritize investments that generate a positive return on investment (ROI). Regularly review your financial performance and adjust your cash flow strategies as needed.

Conclusion

Financing your cargo van and box truck business requires careful planning, research, and strategic decision-making. By exploring diverse funding options and sources, applying for loans and grants effectively, and managing cash flow proactively, you can strengthen your financial position and support sustainable growth.

Evaluate each financing option based on your business goals, risk tolerance, and financial capacity. Seek guidance from financial advisors, mentors, and industry experts to navigate the complexities of business finance and make informed decisions. With a solid financial foundation, you can confidently pursue your entrepreneurial aspirations and build a successful cargo van and box truck business. Let's continue this journey towards achieving your business objectives and securing a prosperous future.

Chapter 7: Setting Up Your Operations

Welcome to Chapter 7 of your journey towards launching your cargo van and box truck business. Setting up your operations involves establishing a functional and efficient infrastructure that supports your day-to-day business activities. In this chapter, we will explore the steps involved in establishing a business location, acquiring necessary equipment and supplies, and setting up office and storage space. By carefully planning and organizing your operational setup, you can create a solid foundation for delivering exceptional service to your customers.

Establishing a Business Location

1. **Choosing a Location:** Selecting the right location for your business is crucial to its success. Consider factors such as proximity to your target market, accessibility for vehicles, availability of parking, and zoning regulations. Evaluate commercial real estate options, lease agreements, and potential growth opportunities in the area.
2. **Leasing or Renting Space:** Decide whether to lease or rent commercial space for your operations. Calculate your budget, rental expenses, and additional costs such as utilities, insurance, and maintenance. Negotiate lease terms that align with your business needs and allow flexibility for future expansion.
3. **Workspace Requirements:** Assess your workspace requirements based on the size of your fleet, number of vehicles, and storage needs for equipment and supplies. Ensure the space is suitable for vehicle maintenance, loading and unloading cargo, and administrative tasks. Consider amenities such as restroom facilities, security features, and internet connectivity.
4. **Obtaining Permits and Licenses:** Obtain necessary permits and licenses for your business location, including zoning permits, occupancy permits, and health department approvals if applicable. Ensure compliance with local regulations and building codes

to operate legally and avoid potential fines or penalties.

Acquiring Necessary Equipment and Supplies

1. **Vehicle Fleet:** Acquire a fleet of cargo vans and box trucks that meet your business requirements. Choose vehicles based on payload capacity, fuel efficiency, reliability, and suitability for different types of deliveries. Consider purchasing or leasing vehicles depending on your financial resources and operational needs.
2. **Equipment and Tools:** Equip your vehicles with necessary tools and equipment for cargo handling, vehicle maintenance, and emergency repairs. This may include hand trucks, dollies, tie-down straps, toolboxes, tire repair kits, and GPS navigation systems. Invest in high-quality equipment to enhance operational efficiency and ensure the safety of your drivers and cargo.
3. **Office Supplies:** Stock up on essential office supplies such as computers, printers, office furniture, stationery, and filing cabinets. Create a designated workspace for administrative tasks, customer service inquiries, and scheduling deliveries. Organize your office space to facilitate productivity and streamline business operations.

4. **Safety and Security Equipment:** Prioritize safety and security by installing necessary equipment such as fire extinguishers, first aid kits, vehicle alarms, and surveillance cameras. Implement safety protocols and training programs to promote a safe working environment for your team and protect your assets from theft or vandalism.

Setting Up Office and Storage Space

1. **Office Layout and Design:** Plan the layout and design of your office space to optimize workflow and functionality. Create designated areas for administrative tasks, customer meetings, and employee break areas. Choose ergonomic furniture and lighting to enhance comfort and productivity for your team members.
2. **Storage and Inventory Management:** Allocate sufficient space for storing inventory, spare parts, and supplies needed for daily operations. Use shelving units, storage racks, and labeling systems to organize inventory efficiently and facilitate easy access. Implement inventory management software to track stock levels, monitor usage patterns, and streamline reordering processes.
3. **Technology Infrastructure:** Establish a reliable technology infrastructure to support your business operations. Set up computer networks, internet

connectivity, and software applications for dispatching, route planning, and customer relationship management (CRM). Invest in cloud-based solutions for data storage, backup, and remote access to support mobile workforce management.

4. **Maintenance Facilities:** If conducting vehicle maintenance in-house, designate a dedicated area for servicing and repairing vehicles. Equip the facility with tools, equipment, and safety measures to comply with industry standards and ensure proper maintenance of your fleet. Establish regular maintenance schedules and inspections to keep vehicles in optimal condition and minimize downtime.

Conclusion

Setting up your operations is a pivotal step in launching and growing your cargo van and box truck business. By strategically establishing a business location, acquiring necessary equipment and supplies, and designing functional office and storage spaces, you can create a solid foundation for operational efficiency and customer satisfaction.

Take the time to research and plan each aspect of your operational setup to align with your business goals and industry standards. Seek guidance from industry experts, suppliers, and business advisors to make informed decisions and optimize your resources effectively.

With a well-organized operational infrastructure in place, you are prepared to deliver reliable transportation services, meet customer expectations, and position your business for long-term success in the competitive marketplace. Let's continue this journey with a commitment to excellence and innovation in your cargo van and box truck operations.

Chapter 8: Hiring and Training Staff

Welcome to Chapter 8 of your journey in establishing your cargo van and box truck business. Hiring and training qualified staff are crucial steps towards building a competent team that drives operational success and delivers exceptional service to your customers. In this chapter, we will explore how to identify staffing needs, implement an effective recruitment and hiring process, and develop comprehensive training and development programs. By investing in your team, you can foster a culture of excellence and ensure the long-term growth and sustainability of your business.

Identifying Staffing Needs

1. **Assess Operational Requirements:** Begin by assessing your operational requirements and identifying the specific roles and responsibilities needed to support daily business operations. Determine the number of drivers, administrative staff, and maintenance personnel required based on the size of your fleet, service offerings, and projected growth.

2. **Skills and Qualifications:** Define the skills, qualifications, and experience necessary for each position within your organization. Consider factors such as driving experience, knowledge of transportation regulations, customer service skills, and proficiency in logistics management software. Outline job descriptions and responsibilities to clarify expectations for potential candidates.
3. **Forecasting Demand:** Forecast future demand for your services and anticipate seasonal fluctuations or peak periods that may require additional staffing. Plan ahead to ensure adequate staffing levels during busy periods while maintaining operational efficiency and meeting customer expectations.
4. **Cultural Fit:** Prioritize cultural fit when evaluating candidates to ensure they align with your company values, work ethic, and commitment to customer satisfaction. Seek individuals who demonstrate teamwork, reliability, and a positive attitude that contributes to a collaborative and supportive work environment.

Recruitment and Hiring Process

1. **Develop a Recruitment Strategy:** Develop a recruitment strategy that outlines sourcing channels, such as job boards, industry associations, social media platforms, and referrals. Leverage networking events,

career fairs, and partnerships with vocational schools or driving academies to attract qualified candidates.

2. **Job Advertising and Outreach:** Create compelling job advertisements that highlight key responsibilities, qualifications, and benefits of working for your company. Use targeted keywords and phrases to attract candidates searching for transportation and logistics opportunities. Promote job openings through online job portals and professional networks to reach a diverse pool of applicants.

3. **Screening and Selection:** Screen resumes and applications to identify candidates who meet your criteria for skills, experience, and cultural fit. Conduct initial phone interviews or video calls to assess candidates' communication skills, professionalism, and interest in the position. Schedule in-person interviews with top candidates to further evaluate their qualifications and suitability for the role.

4. **Conduct Background Checks:** Prior to making a hiring decision, conduct background checks, including driving record checks, criminal background checks, and employment verification. Verify credentials, certifications, and references to ensure candidates meet regulatory requirements and align with your company's standards for safety and professionalism.

Training and Development Programs

1. **Onboarding Process:** Develop a structured onboarding process to introduce new hires to your company culture, policies, and operational procedures. Provide an orientation session that covers safety protocols, job responsibilities, vehicle operation, and customer service expectations. Assign mentors or trainers to support new hires during their initial weeks of employment.
2. **Technical Training:** Offer comprehensive technical training to equip drivers with the skills and knowledge necessary to operate cargo vans and box trucks safely and efficiently. Provide training on vehicle inspection procedures, route planning, navigation systems, and adherence to transportation regulations. Incorporate hands-on training sessions and simulations to reinforce learning and build confidence.
3. **Customer Service Training:** Prioritize customer service training to enhance communication skills, conflict resolution techniques, and responsiveness to customer needs. Emphasize the importance of professionalism, punctuality, and maintaining positive relationships with clients to uphold your company's reputation for reliability and customer satisfaction.
4. **Continuous Learning:** Implement ongoing training and development programs to support employee growth and career advancement within your organization.

Offer opportunities for professional development, such as defensive driving courses, leadership workshops, and certifications in specialized areas of transportation and logistics. Encourage employees to stay updated on industry trends, regulatory changes, and best practices through seminars, webinars, and industry conferences.

Conclusion

Hiring and training staff are integral components of building a successful cargo van and box truck business. By identifying staffing needs, implementing a strategic recruitment process, and investing in comprehensive training and development programs, you can attract top talent, enhance operational efficiency, and deliver superior service to your customers.

Take a proactive approach to staffing by planning for future growth, fostering a positive work environment, and supporting employee success through ongoing learning and professional development. Cultivate a team of dedicated professionals who share your commitment to excellence and contribute to the continued success and expansion of your business.

With a skilled and motivated workforce in place, you are well-positioned to navigate challenges, capitalize on opportunities, and achieve sustainable growth in the competitive transportation and logistics industry. Let's continue this journey with a focus on building a strong, capable team that drives your business forward.

Chapter 9: Developing Your Services

Welcome to Chapter 9 of your journey in establishing your cargo van and box truck business. Developing your services involves defining the types of services you will offer, implementing effective pricing strategies, and creating service packages that meet the diverse needs of your customers. In this chapter, we will explore these key aspects to help you design service offerings that differentiate your business, attract clients, and drive profitability.

Types of Services to Offer

1. **Local Delivery Services:**
   - **Same-Day Delivery:** Offer expedited same-day delivery services for urgent shipments and time-sensitive deliveries within a local area. Cater to businesses and individuals who require fast and reliable transportation solutions.
   - **Last-Mile Delivery:** Provide last-mile delivery services to transport goods from distribution centers or retail stores to customers' doorsteps. Focus on efficiency, accuracy, and customer satisfaction in completing final delivery stages.
2. **Inter-City and Regional Transport:**
   - **Inter-City Transport:** Facilitate inter-city transportation of goods between cities or regions within a specified geographic area. Utilize box trucks for larger cargo

volumes or specialized equipment needed for long-distance hauls.
- **Regional Distribution:** Support regional distribution networks by transporting inventory, supplies, or equipment to satellite locations, warehouses, or retail outlets. Ensure timely deliveries and adherence to delivery schedules to optimize supply chain efficiency.

3. **Specialized Services:**
   - **Fragile or Sensitive Cargo:** Specialize in transporting fragile or sensitive cargo such as electronics, artwork, or medical supplies. Implement handling protocols and protective packaging to ensure safe transport and minimize the risk of damage during transit.
   - **Refrigerated Transport:** Offer refrigerated or temperature-controlled transport services for perishable goods such as food, pharmaceuticals, or floral arrangements. Maintain precise temperature control and compliance with food safety regulations to preserve product integrity.

4. **Contract and Dedicated Services:**
   - **Contract Services:** Establish long-term contracts with businesses or organizations for recurring transportation needs. Provide customized service agreements, dedicated fleet options, and priority scheduling to meet specific client requirements.
   - **Dedicated Services:** Offer dedicated transportation services where vehicles are exclusively assigned to a single client or project. Tailor services to align with client timelines, operational preferences, and service level agreements (SLAs) to foster long-term partnerships.

Pricing Strategies

1. **Cost-Based Pricing:** Determine pricing based on the direct costs associated with each service, including vehicle maintenance, fuel expenses, driver wages, and operational overhead. Calculate a markup or profit margin to ensure profitability while remaining competitive in the market.
2. **Competitive Pricing:** Research competitors' pricing strategies and adjust your rates to reflect market trends, customer expectations, and service differentiation. Position your pricing competitively based on service quality, reliability, and added value features offered to customers.
3. **Value-Based Pricing:** Align pricing with the perceived value of your services to customers. Highlight unique selling propositions (USPs) such as fast delivery times, superior customer service, or specialized handling capabilities. Emphasize the benefits and outcomes clients can expect from choosing your transportation services over alternatives.
4. **Dynamic Pricing:** Implement dynamic pricing strategies based on demand fluctuations, seasonal trends, or peak periods. Adjust rates in real-time to optimize revenue generation, maximize vehicle utilization, and capitalize on high-demand periods while maintaining service quality and customer satisfaction.

1. **Basic Service Packages:** Develop standard service packages that include essential transportation services such as pickup, transport, and delivery. Specify service parameters, delivery timelines, and geographic coverage areas to provide clarity and transparency to customers.
2. **Customizable Options:** Offer customizable service packages that allow clients to tailor transportation solutions to their specific needs and preferences. Provide flexible scheduling, additional service features, or premium options such as expedited delivery or specialized handling at an additional cost.
3. **Tiered Pricing Structure:** Create tiered pricing structures with different service levels or package options to accommodate varying customer budgets and requirements. Offer basic, standard, and premium service tiers with corresponding pricing, service features, and delivery guarantees to cater to diverse clientele.
4. **Bundle Services:** Bundle complementary services or add-on features into comprehensive service packages to enhance value proposition and customer satisfaction. Include options such as packaging, warehousing, insurance coverage, or additional stops to streamline logistics and meet comprehensive transportation needs.

Conclusion

Developing your services is a strategic process that requires careful consideration of service offerings, pricing strategies, and service package development to meet customer expectations and achieve business objectives.

By diversifying your service portfolio, implementing competitive pricing strategies, and creating customizable service packages, you can differentiate your cargo van and box truck business in the competitive transportation industry. Focus on delivering exceptional service quality, building customer trust, and fostering long-term client relationships to drive business growth and profitability.

Continuously evaluate market trends, customer feedback, and industry developments to refine your service offerings and remain agile in responding to evolving customer needs. With a well-defined service strategy in place, you are prepared to capitalize on opportunities, expand your client base, and establish your business as a trusted partner in transportation logistics. Let's continue this journey with a commitment to excellence and innovation in delivering superior transportation solutions to our valued customers.

Chapter 10: Building Your Brand

Welcome to Chapter 10 of your journey in establishing your cargo van and box truck business. Building a strong and recognizable brand is essential for attracting customers, fostering trust, and differentiating your business in the competitive transportation industry. In this chapter, we will explore how to create a compelling brand identity, develop effective marketing materials, and establish a robust online presence. By strategically building your brand, you can enhance visibility, build customer loyalty, and position your business for long-term success.

Creating a Brand Identity

1. **Define Your Brand Values:** Start by defining your brand values, mission statement, and core principles that guide your business operations and customer interactions. Identify what sets your cargo van and box truck business apart from competitors and articulate the unique value proposition (UVP) you offer to clients.
2. **Brand Name and Logo:** Choose a memorable and descriptive name for your business that reflects its purpose and services. Design a professional logo that visually represents your brand identity, incorporating elements such as colors, typography, and symbols that resonate with your target audience. Ensure your logo is versatile and scalable for use across various marketing materials and digital platforms.

3. **Brand Voice and Messaging:** Develop a distinct brand voice that communicates your business personality, values, and tone of communication with customers. Craft compelling messaging that highlights key benefits, service offerings, and customer-centric solutions. Maintain consistency in your brand voice across all communication channels to build brand recognition and trust.
4. **Brand Storytelling:** Share your brand story with customers to create emotional connections and foster authenticity. Highlight the journey, passion, and dedication behind starting your cargo van and box truck business. Showcase customer testimonials, success stories, and case studies that demonstrate your commitment to delivering exceptional service and exceeding client expectations.

Developing Marketing Materials

1. **Business Collateral:** Create professional business collateral including business cards, letterheads, brochures, and flyers that feature your brand name, logo, and contact information. Use high-quality printing materials and design elements that align with your brand aesthetics to leave a lasting impression on potential clients and business partners.
2. **Website Development:** Build a user-friendly and visually appealing website that serves as a central hub

for showcasing your services, customer testimonials, and company information. Include an about us page, service offerings, pricing details, and a contact form for inquiries. Optimize your website for search engines (SEO) to improve online visibility and attract organic traffic.

3. **Digital Marketing Campaigns:** Launch targeted digital marketing campaigns to reach your target audience through online channels such as social media, search engine advertising, and email marketing. Develop engaging content, promotions, and special offers that resonate with prospective clients and encourage them to inquire about your transportation services.

4. **Vehicle Branding:** Utilize vehicle branding and signage to promote your business while on the road. Design eye-catching graphics, logos, and contact information that are prominently displayed on your cargo vans and box trucks. Vehicle wraps and decals serve as mobile advertisements that increase brand visibility and attract potential customers wherever your vehicles travel.

Establishing an Online Presence

1. **Social Media Engagement:** Create and maintain active profiles on popular social media platforms such as Facebook, Instagram, LinkedIn, and Twitter. Share relevant content, industry updates, customer

testimonials, and behind-the-scenes insights to engage with followers and build a community around your brand. Respond promptly to inquiries and reviews to demonstrate customer care and professionalism.

2. **Local Business Listings:** Claim and optimize your business listings on local directories, review sites, and mapping services such as Google My Business, Yelp, and Bing Places. Ensure accurate business information, including address, phone number, website URL, and operating hours, to improve local search visibility and facilitate customer discovery.

3. **Content Marketing Strategy:** Develop a content marketing strategy to establish thought leadership and educate your target audience about transportation logistics and industry trends. Publish informative blog posts, articles, infographics, and videos that address common challenges, offer solutions, and showcase your expertise in delivering reliable transportation services.

4. **Online Reputation Management:** Monitor online reviews, customer feedback, and social media mentions to maintain a positive online reputation. Encourage satisfied clients to leave reviews and testimonials that highlight their experience with your cargo van and box truck services. Address any negative feedback promptly and professionally to demonstrate your commitment to customer satisfaction and continuous improvement.

Conclusion

Building your brand is a strategic process that requires careful planning, creativity, and consistent execution across various marketing channels and customer touchpoints. By creating a compelling brand identity, developing impactful marketing materials, and establishing a strong online presence, you can strengthen brand awareness, attract new customers, and foster long-term loyalty.

Invest in building meaningful relationships with customers, delivering exceptional service experiences, and adapting to market dynamics to sustain brand relevance and competitiveness. With a well-established brand presence and a clear value proposition, you are poised to differentiate your cargo van and box truck business and achieve sustainable growth in the dynamic transportation industry.

Let's continue this journey with enthusiasm and dedication to building a reputable brand that resonates with customers, drives business success, and sets new standards of excellence in transportation logistics.

Chapter 11: Marketing and Promotion

Welcome to Chapter 11 of your journey in establishing your cargo van and box truck business. Effective marketing and promotion are essential for raising awareness, attracting new customers, and expanding your market presence in the competitive transportation industry. In this chapter, we will explore various marketing strategies, tactics, and channels to help you reach your target audience, utilize social media and online advertising effectively, and leverage networking and partnerships to grow your business.

Marketing Strategies and Tactics

1. **Target Audience Identification:** Begin by identifying your target audience—businesses, individuals, or industries that require reliable transportation and logistics services. Segment your audience based on demographics, geographic location, industry sectors, and specific transportation needs to tailor your marketing strategies effectively.
2. **Branding and Differentiation:** Build a strong brand identity that differentiates your cargo van and box truck business from competitors. Highlight your unique value proposition (UVP), key benefits, and competitive advantages such as fast delivery times, customized service options, or specialized handling capabilities. Communicate your brand story and commitment to excellence through all marketing communications.

3. **Content Marketing:** Develop a content marketing strategy to educate, inform, and engage your target audience with valuable and relevant content. Create blog posts, articles, case studies, and infographics that address industry trends, transportation tips, customer success stories, and service updates. Share content across your website, social media platforms, and email newsletters to establish thought leadership and build credibility.
4. **Email Marketing Campaigns:** Launch targeted email marketing campaigns to nurture leads, retain customers, and promote your cargo van and box truck services. Segment your email list based on customer preferences, purchase history, and engagement levels to deliver personalized content, promotional offers, and service updates. Use compelling subject lines, clear calls to action (CTAs), and responsive email templates to optimize campaign performance and drive conversions.

Utilizing Social Media and Online Advertising

1. **Social Media Platforms:** Leverage social media platforms such as Facebook, Instagram, LinkedIn, and Twitter to connect with your target audience, showcase your services, and build relationships. Create engaging posts, share industry insights, customer testimonials, and behind-the-scenes content to

humanize your brand and foster community engagement. Use hashtags, polls, live videos, and interactive stories to increase visibility and encourage user interaction.

2. **Paid Advertising Campaigns:** Invest in targeted online advertising campaigns to reach potential customers and drive traffic to your website or landing pages. Utilize pay-per-click (PPC) advertising on search engines like Google Ads to display ads based on relevant keywords, geographic location, and search intent. Experiment with display ads, retargeting campaigns, and social media ads to expand reach, increase brand awareness, and generate qualified leads.

3. **Search Engine Optimization (SEO):** Optimize your website content, meta tags, and images with relevant keywords and phrases to improve organic search engine rankings. Create valuable, informative, and keyword-rich content that addresses common industry queries and customer pain points. Implement local SEO strategies to enhance visibility in local search results and attract customers searching for transportation services in your area.

4. **Influencer Partnerships:** Collaborate with industry influencers, bloggers, or local businesses to amplify your brand message and reach a broader audience. Partner with influencers who align with your brand values and target demographic to endorse your

services, share promotional offers, or create sponsored content that resonates with their followers. Leverage influencer partnerships to build credibility, increase brand awareness, and drive traffic to your business.

Networking and Partnerships

1. **Industry Associations and Events:** Join industry associations, trade organizations, and networking groups related to transportation, logistics, and business services. Attend industry conferences, seminars, and trade shows to network with industry professionals, potential clients, and business partners. Participate in panel discussions, workshops, and speaking engagements to showcase your expertise and establish credibility within the industry.
2. **Business Referrals:** Cultivate relationships with existing clients, suppliers, and business contacts who can refer new customers to your cargo van and box truck business. Implement a referral program that incentivizes satisfied clients and partners to recommend your services to their networks. Offer discounts, rewards, or exclusive benefits for successful referrals to encourage ongoing word-of-mouth marketing and client acquisition.
3. **Strategic Partnerships:** Form strategic partnerships with complementary businesses, such as logistics providers, ecommerce platforms, manufacturers, or

retailers, to expand service offerings and reach new markets. Collaborate on joint marketing campaigns, cross-promotional activities, or bundled service packages that add value to mutual customers and enhance brand visibility. Establish clear partnership agreements and communication channels to ensure alignment of goals and mutual benefit.

4. **Community Engagement:** Engage with your local community through sponsorship opportunities, charity events, or participation in community initiatives. Demonstrate corporate social responsibility (CSR) by supporting local causes, environmental sustainability efforts, or youth programs that resonate with your brand values. Build positive brand associations and foster goodwill among community members, customers, and stakeholders through active participation and contribution.

Conclusion

Marketing and promotion play a pivotal role in building brand awareness, attracting customers, and driving business growth for your cargo van and box truck operation. By implementing targeted marketing strategies, leveraging social media and online advertising effectively, and cultivating strategic partnerships and networking opportunities, you can establish a strong market presence, differentiate your services, and achieve long-term success in the competitive transportation industry.

Continuously monitor and evaluate marketing performance metrics, customer feedback, and industry trends to refine your marketing strategies and optimize campaign effectiveness. Embrace innovation, adapt to evolving consumer behaviors, and maintain a customer-centric approach to sustain brand relevance and drive sustainable business growth.

With a strategic focus on marketing and promotion, you are well-equipped to expand your client base, increase market share, and position your cargo van and box truck business as a trusted partner in transportation logistics. Let's continue this journey with enthusiasm and dedication to achieving your marketing goals and surpassing customer expectations.

Chapter 12: Sales Strategies

Welcome to Chapter 12 of your journey in establishing your cargo van and box truck business. Developing effective sales strategies is crucial for identifying potential clients, building a robust sales pipeline, closing deals, and maintaining long-term customer relationships. In this chapter, we will explore how to target prospective clients, nurture leads through a structured sales pipeline, and implement strategies to enhance customer retention and satisfaction.

Identifying Potential Clients

1. **Target Market Segmentation:** Begin by identifying your ideal client profile based on industry sectors, business size, geographic location, and transportation needs. Segment potential clients who require reliable and efficient cargo van and box truck services for local deliveries, inter-city transport, or specialized logistics solutions.
2. **Market Research and Analysis:** Conduct market research to identify businesses, industries, or sectors with high demand for transportation services. Analyze market trends, competitive landscape, and customer preferences to pinpoint opportunities and tailor your sales approach to meet specific client needs and challenges.
3. **Networking and Referrals:** Leverage existing relationships, industry contacts, and business referrals

to identify potential clients who may benefit from your transportation services. Attend networking events, industry conferences, and trade shows to connect with decision-makers, procurement officers, and logistics managers who influence purchasing decisions.

4. **Cold Calling and Prospecting:** Develop a proactive approach to prospecting by conducting targeted outreach through cold calling, email campaigns, and direct mail. Research prospects' businesses, identify key pain points or challenges, and personalize your messaging to demonstrate how your services can address their transportation requirements effectively.

Building a Sales Pipeline

1. **Lead Generation:** Generate leads through inbound marketing tactics such as website inquiries, social media engagement, and content downloads. Capture prospect information through lead capture forms, contact forms, and subscription opt-ins to build a database of qualified leads interested in your cargo van and box truck services.
2. **Qualifying Leads:** Qualify leads based on criteria such as budget, timeline, transportation volume, and specific service requirements. Conduct discovery calls or meetings to assess prospects' needs, evaluate fit with your services, and determine their readiness to make a purchasing decision. Prioritize leads that align

with your ideal client profile and demonstrate genuine interest in exploring partnership opportunities.

3. **Sales Presentations and Proposals:** Prepare compelling sales presentations and customized proposals that highlight the benefits, features, and value of your transportation services. Tailor presentations to address client pain points, showcase case studies or testimonials, and provide transparent pricing and service options that align with their budget and operational objectives.

4. **Follow-Up and Nurturing:** Implement a structured follow-up process to maintain momentum and nurture relationships with prospects throughout the sales cycle. Send personalized follow-up emails, schedule follow-up calls, and provide additional information or resources to address lingering questions or objections. Stay proactive in your communication to build trust, demonstrate reliability, and position your business as a preferred transportation partner.

Closing Deals and Maintaining Customer Relationships

1. **Negotiation and Closing Techniques:** Employ effective negotiation techniques to overcome objections, address client concerns, and secure commitment to move forward with your services. Highlight competitive advantages, offer flexible terms or incentives, and negotiate mutually beneficial

agreements that meet client expectations while maximizing profitability for your business.

2. **Contracting and Agreement:** Prepare detailed contracts or service agreements outlining scope of services, pricing terms, delivery schedules, and performance expectations. Ensure contracts are clear, concise, and legally compliant to protect both parties' interests and establish a foundation for a successful business partnership.

3. **Onboarding and Implementation:** Facilitate a smooth onboarding process for new clients by coordinating logistics, scheduling initial deliveries, and introducing key contacts within your organization. Provide comprehensive orientation on service protocols, communication channels, and support resources to ensure clients feel confident and informed from the outset of their partnership with your cargo van and box truck business.

4. **Customer Relationship Management (CRM):** Implement a CRM system to track client interactions, manage sales activities, and monitor progress through the sales pipeline. Use CRM data to personalize client communications, anticipate future needs, and proactively address service issues or opportunities for upselling additional services. Foster ongoing communication and engagement to build strong, long-lasting customer relationships built on trust, reliability, and exceptional service delivery.

Conclusion

Sales strategies are integral to the growth and success of your cargo van and box truck business, enabling you to identify prospective clients, nurture leads, close deals, and cultivate enduring customer relationships. By understanding your target market, building a structured sales pipeline, and implementing effective sales techniques, you can position your business as a trusted transportation partner and drive sustainable revenue growth.

Focus on delivering exceptional value, exceeding client expectations, and continuously refining your sales approach based on market feedback and performance metrics. Embrace a customer-centric mindset, prioritize relationship-building, and adapt to evolving client needs to maintain a competitive edge in the dynamic transportation industry.

With a strategic sales strategy in place, you are well-equipped to capitalize on opportunities, expand your client base, and achieve long-term success in delivering reliable and efficient cargo van and box truck services. Let's continue this journey with confidence and determination to achieve your sales goals and foster lasting partnerships with valued clients.

Chapter 13: Managing Finances

Welcome to Chapter 13 of your journey in establishing your cargo van and box truck business. Effective financial management is critical to the success and sustainability of your operation. In this chapter, we will explore essential practices for bookkeeping, accounting, managing expenses and revenue, as well as financial reporting and analysis. By mastering these aspects, you can make informed decisions, maintain financial health, and support business growth.

Bookkeeping and Accounting

1. **Establishing Financial Systems:** Begin by setting up robust financial systems and processes to track income, expenses, and financial transactions accurately. Use accounting software or cloud-based platforms to streamline bookkeeping tasks, record transactions in real-time, and maintain organized financial records for auditing and tax purposes.
2. **Chart of Accounts:** Develop a comprehensive chart of accounts that categorizes income, expenses, assets, liabilities, and equity specific to your cargo van and box truck business. Customize account codes and categories to align with industry standards, operational costs, and revenue streams associated with transportation services.
3. **Recording Transactions:** Record all financial transactions promptly, including sales invoices, vendor

bills, payroll expenses, fuel costs, vehicle maintenance, and insurance premiums. Maintain supporting documentation such as receipts, invoices, and bank statements to substantiate transactions and facilitate accurate financial reporting.
4. **Reconciling Accounts:** Conduct regular bank reconciliations to ensure accuracy between recorded transactions in your accounting records and bank statements. Verify deposits, withdrawals, and reconciling items to identify discrepancies or errors promptly. Address reconciling differences promptly to maintain the integrity of financial data and prevent financial misstatements.

Managing Expenses and Revenue

1. **Expense Management:** Monitor and control business expenses by categorizing and prioritizing expenditures essential to daily operations, vehicle maintenance, fuel consumption, insurance premiums, and regulatory compliance. Implement cost-saving measures, negotiate favorable terms with suppliers, and review recurring expenses to optimize cash flow and profitability.
2. **Revenue Tracking:** Track revenue generated from transportation services, delivery contracts, recurring service agreements, and one-time shipments. Segment revenue streams by client, service type, and

geographic location to identify profitable services, forecast revenue trends, and allocate resources effectively to support business growth.
3. **Budget Development:** Develop a comprehensive budget that outlines projected income, fixed and variable expenses, capital expenditures, and contingency reserves for unforeseen expenses or market fluctuations. Monitor budget performance regularly, compare actual versus budgeted figures, and adjust spending priorities or revenue targets as needed to achieve financial objectives.
4. **Cash Flow Management:** Manage cash flow effectively by forecasting incoming revenue, monitoring outgoing payments, and maintaining adequate liquidity to cover operational expenses, debt obligations, and investment opportunities. Implement cash flow projections, prioritize accounts receivable collections, and optimize payment schedules to mitigate cash flow gaps and ensure financial stability.

Financial Reporting and Analysis

1. **Financial Statements:** Prepare accurate and timely financial statements including income statements, balance sheets, and cash flow statements to assess business performance, profitability, and financial health. Analyze key financial ratios such as gross profit margin, operating margin, and return on investment

(ROI) to evaluate operational efficiency and financial sustainability.

2. **Financial Performance Metrics:** Monitor key performance indicators (KPIs) such as revenue growth rate, customer acquisition cost (CAC), average revenue per client (ARPC), and profit margins to measure business performance and identify areas for improvement. Compare KPIs against industry benchmarks, historical trends, and competitor performance to gauge market competitiveness and strategic alignment.

3. **Budget Variance Analysis:** Conduct variance analysis to compare actual financial results against budgeted expectations and identify discrepancies or deviations. Investigate underlying factors contributing to budget variances, such as revenue shortfalls, unexpected expenses, or operational inefficiencies. Implement corrective actions and budget adjustments to optimize financial performance and achieve financial goals.

4. **Financial Forecasting:** Utilize financial forecasting techniques to predict future revenue trends, expenses, and cash flow dynamics based on market trends, customer demand, and operational projections. Develop scenario analysis and sensitivity testing to assess the impact of potential changes in business conditions or external factors on financial outcomes. Use forecasts to inform strategic decision-making,

resource allocation, and long-term business planning initiatives.

Conclusion

Managing finances is a foundational aspect of operating a successful cargo van and box truck business, ensuring financial stability, operational efficiency, and long-term sustainability. By implementing sound financial practices, maintaining accurate records, managing expenses and revenue effectively, and leveraging financial reporting and analysis, you can navigate economic uncertainties, capitalize on growth opportunities, and achieve your business objectives.

Commit to continuous improvement in financial management, seek professional advice from financial advisors or accountants as needed, and stay informed about regulatory changes impacting the transportation industry. With a proactive approach to financial management and a focus on data-driven decision-making, you are empowered to optimize profitability, mitigate risks, and drive business growth in the competitive transportation marketplace.

Let's continue this journey with diligence and strategic foresight to build a financially resilient cargo van and box truck business that thrives in dynamic market conditions.

Chapter 14: Implementing Technology

Welcome to Chapter 14 of your journey in establishing your cargo van and box truck business. Embracing technology is essential for optimizing operational efficiency, enhancing service delivery, and maintaining a competitive edge in the transportation industry. In this chapter, we will explore essential software and tools, the utilization of GPS and tracking systems, and strategies for integrating technology into your daily operations to streamline processes and maximize productivity.

Essential Software and Tools

1. **Transportation Management Systems (TMS):** Implement a robust Transportation Management System (TMS) to streamline logistics operations, automate freight management, and optimize route planning and dispatching. TMS software enables you to efficiently manage scheduling, vehicle assignments, load optimization, and real-time communication with drivers and clients. Choose a TMS that integrates with your existing systems and provides scalability to accommodate business growth and evolving customer demands.
2. **Fleet Management Software:** Utilize Fleet Management Software to monitor vehicle performance, track fuel consumption, schedule maintenance tasks, and ensure compliance with

regulatory standards. Fleet management solutions offer real-time visibility into vehicle location, driver behavior, and operational metrics through GPS tracking and telematics. Leverage data analytics and reporting tools to identify cost-saving opportunities, improve fleet efficiency, and mitigate risks associated with vehicle maintenance and operations.

3. **Inventory and Warehouse Management:** Implement Inventory and Warehouse Management software to track inventory levels, manage stock replenishment, and optimize storage space for cargo vans and box trucks. Utilize barcode scanning, RFID technology, or cloud-based inventory systems to streamline order fulfillment, reduce inventory holding costs, and enhance inventory accuracy across multiple locations or distribution centers.

4. **Customer Relationship Management (CRM):** Adopt a Customer Relationship Management (CRM) platform to centralize client interactions, manage customer accounts, and track sales leads and opportunities. CRM software facilitates personalized communication, customer segmentation, and follow-up activities to nurture client relationships and drive repeat business. Integrate CRM with marketing automation tools to streamline lead generation, email campaigns, and customer engagement initiatives.

Utilizing GPS and Tracking Systems

1. **GPS Navigation Systems:** Equip your cargo vans and box trucks with GPS Navigation Systems to optimize route planning, reduce travel time, and minimize fuel consumption. GPS technology provides real-time traffic updates, alternative route suggestions, and navigation assistance to drivers, enhancing efficiency and on-time delivery performance. Integrate GPS with TMS or fleet management software to monitor vehicle location, driver progress, and route adherence for proactive management of logistics operations.
2. **Vehicle Tracking and Telematics:** Implement Vehicle Tracking and Telematics solutions to monitor vehicle health, driver behavior, and operational performance in real-time. Telematics devices capture data on speed, fuel usage, braking patterns, and engine diagnostics to promote safe driving practices, optimize vehicle maintenance schedules, and ensure compliance with regulatory requirements. Leverage telematics insights to improve driver efficiency, reduce operational costs, and enhance overall fleet management strategies.
3. **Asset and Cargo Security:** Enhance asset and cargo security with GPS-enabled tracking devices that monitor shipment status, detect unauthorized movements, and provide geofencing alerts for designated delivery zones. Track valuable assets, high-risk shipments, or sensitive cargo in transit to mitigate

theft risks, ensure chain-of-custody compliance, and safeguard client goods throughout the transportation process.

4. **Driver Performance Monitoring:** Monitor driver performance metrics such as route adherence, idle time, and delivery accuracy using GPS and telematics data. Establish performance benchmarks, provide driver feedback and training opportunities, and incentivize safe driving behaviors to optimize fleet productivity, reduce operational inefficiencies, and uphold service standards for client satisfaction.

Integrating Technology into Your Operations

1. **Workflow Automation:** Streamline operational workflows and task management through automation tools and digital platforms. Implement workflow automation for order processing, dispatching assignments, and service scheduling to minimize manual errors, improve process efficiency, and accelerate service delivery timelines. Integrate automation with TMS or CRM systems to standardize workflows, enhance communication channels, and optimize resource allocation across your organization.
2. **Cloud Computing and Data Analytics:** Leverage Cloud Computing and Data Analytics solutions to store, manage, and analyze large volumes of operational data, customer insights, and performance metrics.

Utilize cloud-based platforms for scalable storage, remote accessibility, and collaborative tools that support real-time decision-making, business intelligence, and predictive analytics. Extract actionable insights from data analytics to identify trends, forecast demand, and drive strategic initiatives for business growth and operational excellence.

3. **Digital Communication Tools:** Enhance internal and external communication with digital collaboration tools, instant messaging platforms, and mobile applications that facilitate real-time communication between dispatchers, drivers, and clients. Utilize communication tools for order updates, delivery notifications, customer inquiries, and service feedback to maintain transparency, responsiveness, and operational agility in dynamic transportation environments.

4. **Cybersecurity and Data Protection:** Prioritize cybersecurity measures and data protection strategies to safeguard sensitive information, client data, and operational systems from cyber threats, data breaches, and unauthorized access. Implement robust cybersecurity protocols, encryption technologies, and access controls to mitigate risks, comply with regulatory requirements, and maintain trust and confidentiality with clients, partners, and stakeholders.

Conclusion

Implementing technology is instrumental in modernizing and optimizing your cargo van and box truck business operations, enhancing efficiency, and delivering superior service to clients. By leveraging essential software and tools, utilizing GPS and tracking systems, and integrating technology into daily workflows, you can streamline logistics processes, improve fleet management, and achieve operational excellence in the competitive transportation industry.

Continuously evaluate technological advancements, adapt to industry trends, and invest in scalable solutions that align with your business objectives and customer expectations. Embrace innovation, empower your team with training and support, and foster a culture of continuous improvement to leverage technology as a strategic asset for sustainable growth, customer satisfaction, and long-term success.

With a strategic approach to technology implementation and a commitment to operational excellence, you are well-positioned to capitalize on opportunities, optimize resource utilization, and drive business innovation in transportation logistics. Let's continue this journey with confidence and determination to harness the power of technology and propel your cargo van and box truck business toward continued success.

Chapter 15: Fleet Management

Welcome to Chapter 15 of your journey in establishing your cargo van and box truck business. Effective fleet management is crucial for ensuring operational efficiency, maintaining vehicle reliability, and delivering exceptional service to your clients. In this chapter, we will explore best practices for maintaining and servicing vehicles, scheduling and dispatching operations, and managing fuel and other operating costs to optimize fleet performance and support business growth.

Maintaining and Servicing Vehicles

1. **Routine Maintenance Schedule:** Develop a proactive maintenance schedule to keep your fleet of cargo vans and box trucks in optimal condition. Schedule regular inspections, oil changes, tire rotations, and brake checks based on manufacturer recommendations and vehicle usage patterns. Implement preventive maintenance to identify potential issues early, minimize downtime, and extend the lifespan of your vehicles.
2. **Vehicle Inspections:** Conduct comprehensive pre-trip and post-trip inspections to ensure vehicle safety, compliance with regulatory standards, and operational readiness. Inspect key components such as brakes, lights, steering, tires, and fluid levels to detect wear and damage that could affect performance or

jeopardize driver safety. Document inspection findings, address maintenance needs promptly, and prioritize repairs to maintain fleet reliability and regulatory compliance.

3. **Emergency Repairs:** Establish protocols for handling emergency repairs and roadside assistance to address unforeseen breakdowns or mechanical failures. Maintain relationships with certified mechanics, towing services, and repair facilities equipped to handle commercial vehicles. Develop contingency plans and communicate emergency procedures to drivers to minimize service interruptions and prioritize vehicle uptime for scheduled deliveries and client commitments.

4. **Vehicle Upgrades and Retrofitting:** Evaluate opportunities for vehicle upgrades, retrofitting, or equipment installations that enhance operational efficiency, safety features, and compliance with environmental regulations. Consider investments in fuel-efficient technologies, GPS tracking systems, ergonomic improvements, or cargo handling equipment that optimize vehicle performance, reduce operating costs, and align with sustainable business practices.

Scheduling and Dispatching

1. **Route Planning and Optimization:** Utilize route planning software or Transportation Management Systems (TMS) to optimize delivery routes, minimize travel distances, and maximize vehicle capacity utilization. Incorporate real-time traffic updates, weather conditions, and customer delivery preferences to enhance route efficiency and ensure on-time deliveries. Communicate route plans and delivery schedules to drivers for proactive navigation and adherence to service commitments.
2. **Dispatching Operations:** Implement efficient dispatching procedures to assign routes, allocate vehicles, and coordinate driver assignments based on workload, geographic coverage, and customer demand. Utilize dispatching software or mobile applications to communicate delivery instructions, update job statuses, and monitor driver locations in real-time. Maintain open communication channels between dispatchers, drivers, and clients to facilitate seamless coordination and responsiveness to changing logistics needs.
3. **Driver Communication and Support:** Establish clear communication protocols and provide ongoing support to drivers regarding route changes, delivery updates, customer inquiries, and operational instructions. Equip drivers with mobile devices, GPS navigation tools, and

access to dispatching systems for real-time communication, route guidance, and emergency assistance. Foster a collaborative environment where drivers can share feedback, report issues, and contribute to continuous improvement initiatives for fleet efficiency and customer satisfaction.

Managing Fuel and Other Operating Costs

1. **Fuel Efficiency Strategies:** Implement fuel management strategies to reduce operating costs and minimize environmental impact. Monitor fuel consumption rates, analyze driving behaviors, and implement fuel-efficient driving techniques such as reduced idling, optimal speed limits, and route optimization. Consider investments in alternative fuels, hybrid vehicles, or electric-powered models to lower fuel expenses, qualify for eco-friendly incentives, and support sustainability initiatives.
2. **Cost Analysis and Budgeting:** Conduct regular cost analysis to track expenditures related to fuel, vehicle maintenance, repairs, insurance premiums, and regulatory compliance. Develop a comprehensive budget that allocates resources for ongoing operational expenses, emergency repairs, and capital investments in fleet expansion or upgrades. Utilize financial forecasting tools to project future costs,

identify cost-saving opportunities, and optimize budget allocation for sustainable business growth.

3. **Vendor Management:** Establish partnerships with fuel suppliers, maintenance providers, and equipment vendors to negotiate favorable terms, discounts, and service agreements that align with your fleet management objectives. Maintain vendor relationships based on reliability, quality of service, and responsiveness to ensure timely fuel deliveries, scheduled maintenance, and cost-effective solutions that support operational continuity and fleet performance metrics.

Conclusion

Effective fleet management is essential for maintaining operational efficiency, maximizing vehicle uptime, and delivering superior service to clients in the competitive transportation industry. By prioritizing vehicle maintenance and servicing, optimizing scheduling and dispatching operations, and managing fuel and operating costs strategically, you can enhance fleet performance, reduce operational expenses, and achieve long-term profitability.

Continuously monitor industry trends, technological advancements, and regulatory changes impacting fleet operations to adapt strategies, improve decision-making, and capitalize on opportunities for innovation and growth. Empower your team with training, resources, and support to uphold service excellence, safety standards, and environmental stewardship in fleet management practices.

With a commitment to continuous improvement and a focus on operational excellence, your cargo van and box truck business is poised to navigate challenges, exceed customer expectations, and sustain success in a dynamic marketplace. Let's continue this journey with diligence and determination to optimize fleet management practices and drive sustainable business outcomes for your transportation enterprise.

Chapter 16: Safety and Compliance

Welcome to Chapter 16 of your journey in establishing your cargo van and box truck business. Safety and compliance are paramount considerations in the transportation industry, ensuring vehicle reliability, driver well-being, and adherence to regulatory standards. In this chapter, we will explore essential practices for ensuring vehicle and driver safety, adhering to transportation regulations, and implementing safety protocols to foster a culture of safety and regulatory compliance within your organization.

Ensuring Vehicle and Driver Safety

1. **Vehicle Maintenance Standards:** Prioritize regular vehicle inspections, maintenance checks, and servicing to uphold safety standards and maximize vehicle

reliability. Implement a proactive maintenance schedule that includes brake inspections, tire rotations, fluid checks, and engine diagnostics to detect and address mechanical issues promptly. Ensure vehicles are equipped with functional safety features, including seat belts, airbags, anti-lock braking systems (ABS), and reflective markings for enhanced visibility during nighttime or adverse weather conditions.

2. **Driver Training and Certification:** Invest in comprehensive driver training programs that emphasize safe driving practices, defensive driving techniques, and regulatory compliance. Provide initial training for new hires and ongoing professional development opportunities to reinforce safety protocols, emergency procedures, and industry best practices. Certify drivers in handling hazardous materials, operating specialized equipment, and complying with transportation regulations to mitigate risks and promote driver competence and confidence on the road.

3. **Safety Inspections and Audits:** Conduct regular safety inspections and audits to assess vehicle condition, equipment functionality, and adherence to safety standards and regulatory requirements. Perform pre-trip and post-trip inspections to verify vehicle readiness, load securement, and compliance with weight restrictions and cargo handling protocols. Document inspection findings, address identified

deficiencies promptly, and implement corrective actions to maintain fleet safety and regulatory compliance.

4. **Emergency Response Preparedness:** Develop and communicate emergency response protocols to drivers for handling accidents, breakdowns, hazardous spills, or adverse weather conditions. Equip vehicles with emergency kits, first aid supplies, and communication devices to facilitate prompt response and assistance during emergencies. Collaborate with local authorities, emergency services, and towing providers to streamline emergency response procedures and ensure driver safety, vehicle recovery, and incident resolution.

Adhering to Transportation Regulations

1. **Regulatory Compliance Awareness:** Stay informed about federal, state, and local transportation regulations, licensing requirements, and industry standards governing commercial vehicle operations. Monitor regulatory updates, attend training seminars, and consult with legal advisors or industry associations to interpret and implement compliance obligations effectively. Maintain accurate records of permits, licenses, vehicle registrations, and compliance certifications to demonstrate regulatory adherence and avoid penalties or sanctions.

2. **Hours of Service (HOS) Compliance:** Monitor and enforce Hours of Service (HOS) regulations to ensure drivers adhere to maximum driving hours, mandatory rest periods, and electronic logging device (ELD) requirements. Implement scheduling tools or TMS software to track driver hours, manage workload distribution, and prevent fatigue-related incidents. Educate drivers on HOS regulations, encourage compliance with duty limits, and prioritize driver well-being to enhance safety and operational efficiency across your fleet.

3. **Cargo Securement and Weight Limits:** Implement rigorous protocols for cargo securement, load distribution, and compliance with weight limits to prevent shifting loads, vehicle instability, and road hazards during transit. Utilize proper tie-down methods, load restraint systems, and cargo securing devices that comply with Federal Motor Carrier Safety Administration (FMCSA) guidelines and industry best practices. Train drivers in proper load handling techniques, conduct regular inspections of cargo loads, and enforce safety measures to protect against load-related accidents and regulatory violations.

4. **Environmental and Emission Compliance:** Ensure compliance with environmental regulations, emissions standards, and sustainability initiatives applicable to your fleet operations. Monitor vehicle emissions, implement maintenance practices that reduce carbon

footprint, and consider investments in eco-friendly technologies or alternative fuels to minimize environmental impact. Participate in industry programs, adopt green practices, and promote environmental stewardship to align with regulatory requirements and community expectations for sustainable transportation practices.

Implementing Safety Protocols

1. **Safety Policies and Procedures:** Develop comprehensive safety policies, procedures, and operational guidelines that prioritize driver safety, vehicle maintenance, and regulatory compliance. Communicate safety expectations, roles, and responsibilities to employees, contractors, and third-party service providers to foster a culture of safety awareness and accountability. Conduct regular safety meetings, training sessions, and performance reviews to reinforce safety protocols, address concerns, and promote continuous improvement in safety performance metrics.
2. **Incident Reporting and Investigation:** Establish protocols for reporting and investigating safety incidents, near misses, or hazardous conditions to identify root causes, implement corrective actions, and prevent recurrence. Encourage open communication channels for reporting safety concerns, implementing

corrective actions, and fostering a proactive safety culture within your organization. Document incident reports, analyze trends in safety data, and collaborate with stakeholders to implement preventive measures that enhance workplace safety and mitigate risks to personnel and assets.

3. **Driver Wellness and Support:** Prioritize driver wellness initiatives, mental health awareness, and support programs to promote physical well-being, emotional resilience, and work-life balance among your workforce. Provide access to wellness resources, counseling services, and employee assistance programs (EAPs) to support drivers' overall health and reduce stress-related factors that may impact job performance or safety on the road. Foster a supportive work environment, encourage open dialogue, and recognize drivers for their contributions to safety and operational excellence.

Conclusion

Safety and compliance are integral to the success and reputation of your cargo van and box truck business, ensuring vehicle reliability, driver well-being, and regulatory adherence in the transportation industry. By prioritizing vehicle and driver safety, adhering to transportation regulations, and implementing robust safety protocols, you can mitigate risks, enhance operational efficiency, and uphold industry standards for customer satisfaction and stakeholder trust.

Continuously assess safety performance metrics, leverage technology for monitoring and compliance purposes, and engage stakeholders in safety initiatives to cultivate a culture of safety excellence and continuous improvement. Embrace innovation, invest in driver training and support, and collaborate with regulatory authorities and industry partners to navigate evolving safety challenges and sustain a safe, compliant, and resilient fleet operation.

With a commitment to safety leadership and regulatory compliance, your cargo van and box truck business is poised for sustainable growth, operational success, and industry leadership in delivering safe, reliable transportation services. Let's continue this journey with vigilance and dedication to achieving safety excellence and driving positive outcomes for your organization and the communities you serve.

Chapter 17: Customer Service Excellence

Welcome to Chapter 17 of your journey in establishing your cargo van and box truck business. Customer service excellence is not just about meeting client expectations; it's about exceeding them consistently, building trust, and fostering long-term relationships. In this chapter, we will explore strategies for providing exceptional customer service, handling customer complaints and feedback effectively, and cultivating strong, enduring relationships with your clients to drive business success and customer loyalty.

Providing Exceptional Customer Service

1. **Clear Communication:** Establish clear communication channels and practices to ensure transparency, responsiveness, and proactive engagement with clients. Communicate service offerings, delivery timelines, pricing details, and terms of service clearly and concisely to manage client expectations and build trust from the outset. Utilize customer relationship management (CRM) systems or communication platforms to maintain open lines of communication, provide timely updates, and address client inquiries or concerns promptly.
2. **Personalized Service:** Tailor service offerings to meet individual client needs, preferences, and unique business requirements. Listen actively to client feedback, understand their challenges, and offer

customized solutions or value-added services that align with their goals and operational priorities. Demonstrate a genuine interest in client success, anticipate their evolving needs, and proactively propose opportunities for service enhancement or collaboration to deliver personalized experiences that differentiate your business in the marketplace.

3. **Timely Response and Resolution:** Prioritize responsiveness and timely resolution of client inquiries, service requests, or issues to demonstrate reliability, professionalism, and commitment to customer satisfaction. Establish service level agreements (SLAs) or response time expectations for handling customer communications, resolving complaints, and addressing operational concerns promptly. Empower customer service representatives with training, resources, and authority to expedite issue resolution and uphold service standards that exceed client expectations.

Handling Customer Complaints and Feedback

1. **Active Listening:** Practice active listening skills to understand the root cause of customer complaints, validate their concerns, and demonstrate empathy and understanding. Encourage clients to express their feedback openly, without interruption, and acknowledge their perspectives to foster trust and

rapport. Ask clarifying questions, summarize key points, and seek mutual agreement on resolution steps to address grievances effectively and restore client confidence in your service delivery.

2. **Resolution Strategies:** Implement structured processes and escalation procedures for handling customer complaints, service disruptions, or quality issues with professionalism and accountability. Investigate complaints thoroughly, gather relevant information, and collaborate cross-functionally to identify corrective actions, prevent recurrence, and implement service improvements that align with client expectations. Communicate resolution timelines, updates, and follow-up actions transparently to keep clients informed and engaged throughout the resolution process.

3. **Service Recovery:** Proactively engage in service recovery efforts by offering apologies, rectifying errors promptly, and compensating clients appropriately for service shortcomings or inconveniences. Empower frontline staff with authority to resolve issues swiftly, escalate complex cases as needed, and prioritize client satisfaction in every interaction. Turn negative experiences into opportunities for relationship-building by demonstrating commitment to service excellence, responsiveness to feedback, and dedication to continuous improvement in customer service delivery.

1. **Relationship Building Initiatives:** Invest in relationship-building initiatives, loyalty programs, or client appreciation gestures to recognize and reward long-term clients for their trust and continued partnership. Personalize communication, celebrate milestones, and express gratitude through personalized notes, exclusive offers, or invitations to client appreciation events that reinforce your commitment to their success and strengthen emotional connections with your brand.
2. **Feedback Collection and Analysis:** Proactively solicit client feedback through surveys, satisfaction assessments, or feedback mechanisms to gather insights, measure service performance, and identify opportunities for service enhancement. Analyze feedback trends, prioritize action items, and communicate improvement initiatives transparently to demonstrate responsiveness to client input and reinforce a culture of continuous improvement in customer service excellence.
3. **Customer Education and Support:** Provide ongoing education, training resources, or industry insights to empower clients with knowledge, best practices, and operational strategies that add value to their business operations. Offer proactive support, troubleshooting assistance, or access to subject matter experts to

address client inquiries, optimize service utilization, and foster self-sufficiency in leveraging your services to achieve their business objectives.

Conclusion

Customer service excellence is a cornerstone of your cargo van and box truck business, driving customer satisfaction, retention, and competitive differentiation in the transportation industry. By prioritizing clear communication, personalized service delivery, and proactive resolution of customer concerns, you can build trust, loyalty, and advocacy among your clients. Embrace feedback as a catalyst for continuous improvement, invest in relationship-building initiatives, and empower your team to deliver exceptional customer experiences that exceed expectations and sustain long-term business success.

Nurture client relationships with integrity, responsiveness, and a commitment to service excellence that distinguishes your brand in a crowded marketplace. Celebrate successes, learn from challenges, and evolve your customer service strategies to align with evolving client needs and industry trends. With dedication to fostering enduring customer relationships, your cargo van and box truck business is poised to thrive, grow, and lead with excellence in delivering value-driven transportation solutions to clients worldwide. Let's continue this journey with passion and purpose to achieve unparalleled customer service excellence and elevate your business to new heights of success.

3.5

Write an entire chapter on next Chapter 18: Scaling Your Business Expanding your fleet Adding new services and markets Managing growth and scalability, write 3,000 characters make it detailed in a friendly human way

ChatGPT

Chapter 18: Scaling Your Business

Welcome to Chapter 18 of your journey in building and expanding your cargo van and box truck business. Scaling your business involves strategic growth initiatives, expanding your fleet, diversifying services, and entering new markets to capitalize on opportunities and sustain long-term success. In this chapter, we will explore essential strategies for scaling your business effectively, managing growth, and enhancing scalability to accommodate increasing demands and achieve your business expansion goals.

Expanding Your Fleet

1. **Assessing Fleet Needs:** Conduct a comprehensive assessment of current operational capacity, client demand, and market trends to determine optimal fleet expansion strategies. Evaluate factors such as service volume, geographic coverage, and seasonal

fluctuations in demand to forecast future fleet requirements accurately. Consider financial feasibility, capital investment, and operational efficiencies when planning fleet expansion initiatives to align with business objectives and support sustainable growth.

2. **Acquiring New Vehicles:** Research and select vehicle models that align with operational requirements, client preferences, and industry standards for reliability, performance, and fuel efficiency. Explore options for purchasing or leasing new vehicles, considering factors such as upfront costs, financing terms, depreciation rates, and maintenance expenses. Negotiate favorable terms with suppliers, manufacturers, or dealerships to maximize value and minimize acquisition costs while maintaining fleet quality and operational readiness.

3. **Integration and Fleet Management:** Implement scalable fleet management solutions, such as GPS tracking systems, telematics technology, or fleet management software, to monitor vehicle performance, optimize route planning, and enhance operational efficiency. Streamline integration processes, onboard new vehicles efficiently, and train drivers on operating procedures, safety protocols, and compliance requirements to ensure seamless integration of expanded fleet capacity into daily operations.

1. **Market Research and Analysis:** Conduct market research to identify emerging opportunities, client needs, and competitive dynamics in new service sectors or geographic markets. Analyze industry trends, customer preferences, and regulatory requirements to assess market viability and potential demand for expanded service offerings. Develop targeted marketing strategies, sales initiatives, and promotional campaigns to introduce new services effectively and penetrate untapped market segments.

2. **Diversifying Service Offerings:** Expand service capabilities by introducing complementary services, value-added solutions, or specialized service packages that align with client expectations and market demand. Customize service offerings to cater to specific industry sectors, operational requirements, or niche markets to differentiate your business and create competitive advantages. Leverage cross-selling opportunities, bundle services strategically, and promote integrated solutions to maximize revenue streams and enhance client satisfaction.

3. **Entering New Markets:** Evaluate expansion opportunities in new geographic regions, urban centers, or demographic segments where demand for transportation services is growing or underserved. Conduct feasibility studies, assess regulatory

compliance, and establish local partnerships or distribution channels to facilitate market entry and navigate cultural, logistical, or operational challenges effectively. Adapt business strategies, pricing models, and service delivery approaches to align with regional market dynamics and capitalize on growth opportunities.

Managing Growth and Scalability

1. **Business Planning and Forecasting:** Develop a comprehensive business plan that outlines growth objectives, financial projections, and strategic milestones for scaling your business operations. Establish measurable goals, performance metrics, and key performance indicators (KPIs) to track progress, monitor business performance, and evaluate the success of growth initiatives. Conduct regular reviews, scenario planning, and risk assessments to anticipate challenges, mitigate risks, and optimize resource allocation for sustainable growth.
2. **Operational Efficiency and Optimization:** Implement lean management principles, process improvements, and automation technologies to enhance operational efficiency, streamline workflows, and reduce overhead costs associated with business expansion. Standardize operational procedures, leverage scalable infrastructure, and invest in training programs to

empower employees, optimize productivity, and maintain service quality amidst growing operational demands.

3. **Financial Management and Resource Allocation:** Manage financial resources prudently by establishing budgetary controls, monitoring cash flow, and optimizing capital expenditures to support growth initiatives without compromising financial stability. Seek financing options, investment opportunities, or strategic partnerships to fund expansion projects, acquire capital assets, and capitalize on growth opportunities while maintaining liquidity and financial resilience in dynamic market conditions.

Conclusion

Scaling your cargo van and box truck business requires strategic foresight, proactive planning, and a commitment to operational excellence to achieve sustainable growth and competitive advantage in the transportation industry. By expanding your fleet capacity, diversifying service offerings, and entering new markets strategically, you can capitalize on market opportunities, meet evolving client needs, and position your business for long-term success.

Embrace innovation, leverage technology-driven solutions, and foster a culture of continuous improvement to optimize operational efficiency, enhance scalability, and drive profitability in your business expansion efforts. Monitor industry trends, customer feedback, and competitive dynamics to adapt strategies, innovate service delivery, and maintain agility in responding to market changes and customer expectations.

With a steadfast focus on strategic growth initiatives, operational excellence, and client-centric service delivery, your cargo van and box truck business is poised to scale new heights, expand market presence, and achieve sustainable business growth. Let's continue this journey with determination and vision to unlock new opportunities, overcome challenges, and realize your aspirations for business expansion and industry leadership.

Chapter 19: Managing Risks

Welcome to Chapter 19 of your journey in establishing and growing your cargo van and box truck business. Managing risks is essential for safeguarding your operations, protecting assets, and ensuring continuity amidst unforeseen challenges. In this chapter, we will explore strategies for identifying potential risks, developing a comprehensive risk management plan, and addressing insurance and liability considerations to mitigate risks effectively and promote business resilience.

Identifying Potential Risks

1. **Operational Risks:** Assess operational risks associated with daily business activities, including vehicle breakdowns, equipment failure, driver shortages, or disruptions in supply chain logistics. Identify vulnerabilities in service delivery, fleet management, or operational processes that may impact business continuity, client satisfaction, or regulatory compliance. Conduct risk assessments, site inspections, and operational audits to evaluate potential hazards, mitigate operational risks, and implement preventive measures to minimize downtime and service interruptions.
2. **Financial Risks:** Evaluate financial risks, such as fluctuating fuel prices, currency exchange rates, inflationary pressures, or economic downturns that

may affect profitability, cash flow, or capital investment decisions. Monitor market trends, financial indicators, and economic forecasts to anticipate financial risks, establish contingency plans, and optimize financial strategies for managing liquidity, debt obligations, and revenue diversification amidst market volatility.

3. **Compliance and Regulatory Risks:** Stay informed about regulatory changes, licensing requirements, environmental regulations, and transportation laws that govern commercial vehicle operations. Monitor compliance with industry standards, safety regulations, and emissions controls to mitigate regulatory risks, avoid penalties, and uphold legal obligations. Implement compliance monitoring programs, training initiatives, and internal controls to ensure adherence to regulatory requirements and foster a culture of regulatory compliance within your organization.

Developing a Risk Management Plan

1. **Risk Identification and Assessment:** Conduct a thorough risk assessment to identify, prioritize, and quantify potential risks based on their impact and likelihood of occurrence. Collaborate with stakeholders, subject matter experts, and industry advisors to gather insights, analyze risk exposure, and develop risk registers that document identified risks,

root causes, and potential consequences for informed decision-making and risk mitigation planning.
2. **Risk Mitigation Strategies:** Implement risk mitigation strategies, control measures, and action plans to minimize identified risks, mitigate their impact, and enhance business resilience. Prioritize high-risk areas, implement preventive controls, and establish contingency plans to respond promptly to emergencies, crisis situations, or unforeseen events that may threaten business operations, stakeholder interests, or client relationships. Continuously monitor risk indicators, adjust mitigation strategies, and communicate risk management efforts transparently to stakeholders to foster confidence in your risk management practices.
3. **Business Continuity Planning:** Develop a business continuity plan (BCP) that outlines procedures, protocols, and recovery strategies for maintaining essential business functions, restoring operations, and minimizing disruption in the event of a crisis, natural disaster, or operational setback. Identify critical resources, alternative suppliers, and emergency response protocols to facilitate timely recovery, protect assets, and ensure uninterrupted service delivery to clients while mitigating financial, operational, and reputational risks.

Insurance and Liability Considerations

1. **Insurance Coverage:** Evaluate insurance options, coverage limits, and policy exclusions to protect against potential liabilities, property damage, bodily injury, or third-party claims arising from business operations. Obtain comprehensive insurance coverage tailored to commercial vehicle operations, including commercial auto insurance, general liability insurance, cargo insurance, and worker's compensation coverage to mitigate financial risks, legal liabilities, and unforeseen expenses associated with accidents, property damage, or legal disputes.
2. **Liability Management:** Implement risk transfer strategies, contractual agreements, and indemnification clauses to allocate and manage liability exposure effectively in business contracts, vendor relationships, and client engagements. Establish risk management protocols, safety protocols, and emergency response procedures to minimize liability risks, protect corporate assets, and promote compliance with contractual obligations, industry standards, and legal requirements.
3. **Claims Management and Incident Response:** Develop protocols for managing insurance claims, incident reporting, and claims resolution processes to facilitate prompt response, documentation, and resolution of insurance claims, accidents, or incidents affecting

business operations. Collaborate with insurance providers, legal advisors, and claims adjusters to expedite claims processing, negotiate settlements, and mitigate financial losses associated with insurance claims, legal disputes, or liability claims filed against your business.

Conclusion

Managing risks is integral to sustaining operational excellence, safeguarding business continuity, and protecting the long-term viability of your cargo van and box truck business. By proactively identifying potential risks, developing a comprehensive risk management plan, and addressing insurance and liability considerations, you can mitigate operational vulnerabilities, optimize risk exposure, and enhance resilience against unforeseen challenges.

Embrace a proactive approach to risk management, integrate risk mitigation strategies into daily operations, and foster a culture of accountability, compliance, and continuous improvement to safeguard business assets, protect stakeholder interests, and uphold client trust. Monitor emerging risks, adapt risk management strategies to evolving market conditions, and leverage industry insights, technology solutions, and best practices to mitigate risks effectively and drive sustainable growth in your business.

With a commitment to proactive risk management practices, strategic foresight, and resilience-building initiatives, your cargo van and box truck business is well-positioned to navigate uncertainties, capitalize on opportunities, and achieve long-term success in the competitive transportation industry. Let's continue this journey with vigilance, preparedness, and confidence to mitigate risks, maximize business potential, and sustain operational excellence in delivering value-driven transportation solutions to clients worldwide.

Chapter 20: Sustainability and Environmental Responsibility

Welcome to Chapter 20 of your journey in establishing and growing your cargo van and box truck business. Embracing sustainability and environmental responsibility not only enhances your business reputation but also contributes to a cleaner, healthier planet. In this chapter, we will explore strategies for implementing eco-friendly practices, reducing your carbon footprint, and promoting sustainability within your business operations to align with environmental goals and stakeholder expectations.

Implementing Eco-Friendly Practices

1. **Fuel Efficiency Initiatives:** Invest in fuel-efficient vehicles, hybrid or electric models, and alternative fuel technologies to reduce greenhouse gas emissions, lower fuel costs, and enhance operational efficiency.

Monitor vehicle performance, optimize route planning, and promote eco-driving techniques among drivers to maximize fuel efficiency, minimize environmental impact, and support sustainable transportation practices. Implement maintenance schedules, tune-ups, and vehicle inspections to ensure optimal engine performance and fuel economy across your fleet.

2. **Vehicle Maintenance and Emissions Control:** Adhere to regular maintenance schedules, emissions testing, and compliance with environmental regulations to reduce vehicle emissions, air pollutants, and environmental impact associated with fleet operations. Implement emission reduction strategies, upgrade vehicle systems, and adopt emission control technologies to achieve compliance with emission standards, mitigate environmental risks, and improve air quality in communities served by your transportation services.

3. **Waste Management and Recycling Programs:** Establish waste reduction initiatives, recycling programs, and sustainable procurement practices to minimize waste generation, promote resource conservation, and divert recyclable materials from landfill disposal. Implement recycling bins, waste segregation policies, and eco-friendly packaging solutions to reduce environmental footprint, conserve natural resources, and support circular economy

principles within your business operations and supply chain logistics.

Reducing Your Carbon Footprint

1. **Carbon Offsetting Programs:** Participate in carbon offsetting programs, renewable energy projects, or tree-planting initiatives to offset carbon emissions generated by business operations, vehicle fleet, and transportation activities. Collaborate with environmental organizations, carbon offset providers, or sustainability partners to calculate carbon footprint, purchase carbon credits, and invest in environmental projects that contribute to global carbon neutrality goals, biodiversity conservation, and climate resilience initiatives.
2. **Energy Efficiency and Conservation:** Adopt energy-efficient lighting, heating, ventilation, and air conditioning (HVAC) systems, and implement energy conservation measures to reduce energy consumption, lower utility costs, and minimize greenhouse gas emissions associated with facility operations. Conduct energy audits, implement energy-saving technologies, and educate employees on energy conservation practices to foster a culture of sustainability, reduce environmental impact, and achieve operational efficiency goals.

3. **Supply Chain Sustainability:** Evaluate suppliers, vendors, and business partners based on environmental sustainability criteria, ethical sourcing practices, and commitment to corporate social responsibility (CSR) principles. Collaborate with sustainable suppliers, source eco-friendly materials, and prioritize products with minimal environmental footprint to promote sustainability throughout your supply chain, reduce ecological impact, and support responsible consumption and production practices in global markets.

Promoting Sustainability in Your Business

1. **Stakeholder Engagement and Education:** Engage employees, stakeholders, and community members through sustainability initiatives, educational workshops, and awareness campaigns to raise awareness about environmental issues, promote sustainable practices, and encourage participation in corporate sustainability programs. Foster a culture of environmental stewardship, empower employees to contribute to sustainability goals, and recognize achievements in sustainability leadership to inspire collective action and drive positive change within your organization.
2. **Transparency and Reporting:** Commit to transparency in reporting environmental performance, sustainability

metrics, and progress towards sustainability goals to stakeholders, regulatory authorities, and industry peers. Publish annual sustainability reports, disclose environmental impacts, and communicate sustainability initiatives, achievements, and challenges transparently to build trust, accountability, and credibility as a responsible corporate citizen committed to environmental stewardship and sustainable business practices.

3. **Continuous Improvement and Innovation:** Embrace innovation, research, and development of sustainable technologies, renewable energy solutions, and eco-friendly innovations to drive continuous improvement, optimize resource efficiency, and pioneer sustainable practices in the transportation industry. Collaborate with industry partners, academia, and research institutions to advance sustainability initiatives, pilot green technologies, and leverage data-driven insights to innovate sustainable solutions that enhance business competitiveness and environmental resilience.

Conclusion

Sustainability and environmental responsibility are integral to the future success, resilience, and reputation of your cargo van and box truck business in a global economy increasingly focused on environmental conservation and climate action.

By implementing eco-friendly practices, reducing your carbon footprint, and promoting sustainability within your business operations, you can mitigate environmental impact, foster stakeholder trust, and contribute to a more sustainable future for generations to come.

Embrace sustainability as a core value, integrate environmental stewardship into business strategies, and lead by example in adopting responsible business practices that prioritize planet, people, and prosperity. Monitor industry trends, collaborate with sustainability partners, and leverage innovation to drive positive environmental impact, achieve sustainability goals, and position your business as a leader in sustainable transportation solutions. Together, we can create a greener, more sustainable world while driving business success and societal progress through responsible environmental leadership and commitment to sustainable development goals.

Chapter 21: Networking and Building Relationships

Welcome to Chapter 21 of your journey in establishing and growing your cargo van and box truck business. Networking and building relationships are essential strategies for expanding your professional connections, fostering industry collaborations, and gaining valuable insights to support business growth and development. In this chapter, we will explore effective networking techniques, the benefits of joining industry associations, building partnerships, and leveraging industry events to strengthen your business network and enhance your competitive edge in the transportation industry.

Joining Industry Associations and Groups

1. **Benefits of Membership:** Joining industry associations, trade groups, and professional organizations provides valuable networking opportunities, industry insights, and access to resources that can benefit your business. Membership offers opportunities to connect with industry peers, share best practices, and stay informed about regulatory changes, industry trends, and emerging technologies shaping the transportation sector. Engage in association activities, committee involvement, and leadership roles to expand your network, establish thought leadership, and influence industry standards that impact your business operations.

2. **Networking Events and Workshops:** Attend networking events, workshops, and educational seminars hosted by industry associations to network with industry leaders, business professionals, and subject matter experts. Participate in networking sessions, panel discussions, and knowledge-sharing forums to exchange ideas, build relationships, and collaborate on industry initiatives that promote professional development, business growth, and industry innovation. Leverage networking opportunities to identify potential partners, explore collaboration opportunities, and cultivate strategic alliances that enhance your business capabilities and market presence.
3. **Access to Resources and Support:** Utilize association resources, member benefits, and industry publications to access research reports, market intelligence, and industry data that inform business decision-making, strategic planning, and operational improvements. Leverage educational resources, training programs, and certification opportunities offered by industry associations to enhance employee skills, professional competencies, and industry knowledge within your organization. Engage with association mentors, advisors, and industry experts to seek guidance, mentorship, and practical insights that support business growth, leadership development, and

organizational success in the competitive transportation marketplace.

Building Partnerships and Alliances

1. **Identifying Strategic Partners:** Identify potential partners, suppliers, and strategic alliances within the transportation ecosystem that complement your business strengths, expand service capabilities, or enhance market reach. Evaluate partnership opportunities based on shared values, mutual interests, and strategic alignment to foster collaborative relationships, achieve common goals, and capitalize on synergies that drive business growth, innovation, and competitive advantage. Establish partnership criteria, conduct due diligence, and negotiate partnership agreements that outline roles, responsibilities, and expectations to ensure alignment, transparency, and accountability in collaborative ventures.
2. **Collaborative Projects and Initiatives:** Collaborate with industry partners, technology providers, or logistics stakeholders on joint projects, innovation initiatives, or pilot programs that leverage complementary strengths, expertise, and resources to address industry challenges, explore new markets, or introduce innovative solutions that enhance operational efficiency and customer value. Participate

in industry consortia, public-private partnerships, or collaborative networks that facilitate knowledge sharing, industry collaboration, and collective action on sustainability, regulatory compliance, or market development initiatives that benefit your business and contribute to industry advancement.

3. **Strategic Alliances and Market Expansion:** Form strategic alliances, distribution agreements, or joint ventures with industry leaders, market influencers, or global partners to expand market presence, enter new geographic regions, or diversify service offerings that align with market demand, customer preferences, and business growth objectives. Leverage alliance networks, cross-promotion opportunities, and collaborative marketing strategies to amplify brand visibility, enhance market positioning, and capitalize on shared resources, expertise, and market access to achieve sustainable business expansion and competitive differentiation in the dynamic transportation marketplace.

Attending Industry Events and Conferences

1. **Professional Networking Opportunities:** Attend industry conferences, trade shows, and business expositions to network with industry stakeholders, prospective clients, and key decision-makers from across the transportation sector. Engage in networking

receptions, industry mixers, and exhibitor showcases to establish meaningful connections, cultivate business relationships, and explore collaboration opportunities that support business development, client acquisition, and market expansion initiatives. Exchange contact information, follow up with new contacts, and nurture relationships through ongoing communication, mutual support, and shared interests that foster long-term partnerships and business success.

2. **Knowledge Sharing and Thought Leadership:** Participate in conference sessions, keynote presentations, and industry panels featuring thought leaders, subject matter experts, and industry influencers who share insights, trends, and best practices shaping the future of transportation. Gain industry intelligence, market perspectives, and strategic insights that inform business strategy, innovation initiatives, and decision-making processes to anticipate market trends, capitalize on emerging opportunities, and navigate industry challenges with confidence and foresight. Contribute to thought leadership discussions, share industry expertise, and showcase business achievements to build credibility, influence industry discourse, and establish your business as a trusted leader in the transportation marketplace.

3. **Business Development and Partnership Exploration:** Explore business development opportunities,

partnership prospects, and collaborative ventures through scheduled meetings, networking sessions, or matchmaking programs facilitated by conference organizers. Initiate conversations, exchange business proposals, and explore synergistic opportunities with potential partners, investors, or technology providers interested in supporting your business growth, expanding market reach, or advancing innovation initiatives that enhance operational efficiency, customer satisfaction, and competitive advantage in the competitive transportation landscape.

Conclusion

Networking and building relationships are foundational strategies for advancing your cargo van and box truck business, fostering industry connections, and positioning your organization for sustained growth and success in the dynamic transportation marketplace. By joining industry associations, building strategic partnerships, and participating in industry events, you can expand your professional network, leverage collaborative opportunities, and access valuable resources, insights, and expertise that drive business innovation, enhance market competitiveness, and accelerate achievement of your business goals.

Embrace networking as a strategic imperative, cultivate meaningful relationships, and actively engage in industry communities, forums, and collaborative initiatives that promote knowledge sharing, industry collaboration, and collective action on shared priorities that impact your business and the transportation industry at large. With a proactive approach to relationship-building, collaboration, and industry engagement, your cargo van and box truck business can forge new pathways to success, seize growth opportunities, and achieve sustainable business growth while contributing to industry advancement and leadership in the evolving transportation landscape.

Chapter 22: Leveraging Data and Analytics

Welcome to Chapter 22 of your journey in establishing and growing your cargo van and box truck business. In today's digital age, leveraging data and analytics is crucial for optimizing business performance, making informed decisions, and driving continuous improvement initiatives. In this chapter, we will explore strategies for tracking and analyzing business performance, utilizing data-driven insights to enhance decision-making processes, and implementing continuous improvement strategies that drive operational efficiency, customer satisfaction, and business growth in the competitive transportation industry.

Tracking and Analyzing Business Performance

1. **Key Performance Indicators (KPIs):** Identify and track key performance indicators (KPIs) that measure critical aspects of your business operations, such as fleet utilization rates, vehicle maintenance costs, delivery times, customer satisfaction levels, and revenue per mile. Establish performance benchmarks, set measurable goals, and track KPI metrics regularly to monitor business performance, identify trends, and assess operational efficiency, productivity, and profitability across your cargo van and box truck fleet. Utilize performance dashboards, data visualization tools, and KPI reports to gain actionable insights, identify performance gaps, and prioritize improvement

initiatives that optimize business outcomes and drive sustainable growth.

2. **Operational Efficiency Analysis:** Conduct operational efficiency analysis, route optimization studies, and vehicle performance evaluations to identify opportunities for cost reduction, fuel savings, and operational improvements within your transportation operations. Utilize historical performance data, GPS tracking systems, and route planning software to analyze delivery routes, minimize mileage, reduce idle time, and optimize vehicle scheduling to enhance operational efficiency, reduce transportation costs, and improve overall fleet performance metrics. Implement operational best practices, standard operating procedures (SOPs), and performance improvement initiatives to streamline workflow processes, maximize resource utilization, and achieve operational excellence in delivering quality transportation services to clients.

3. **Customer Insights and Feedback:** Collect customer feedback, conduct satisfaction surveys, and analyze customer service metrics to gain insights into customer preferences, expectations, and satisfaction levels with your transportation services. Utilize customer relationship management (CRM) systems, feedback mechanisms, and service quality metrics to measure customer loyalty, retention rates, and overall satisfaction with service delivery. Incorporate

customer feedback into business decision-making processes, service enhancements, and operational improvements to address customer needs, exceed service expectations, and foster long-term customer relationships that drive business growth and competitive advantage in the transportation marketplace.

Utilizing Data to Make Informed Decisions

1. **Data-driven Decision Making:** Embrace a data-driven approach to decision-making by leveraging data analytics, predictive modeling, and business intelligence tools to generate actionable insights, assess risk factors, and evaluate strategic alternatives that optimize business performance and support informed decision-making processes. Analyze market trends, customer behavior patterns, and operational data to identify growth opportunities, mitigate business risks, and align business strategies with evolving market dynamics, competitive pressures, and industry trends that impact your cargo van and box truck business operations. Utilize data visualization techniques, trend analysis reports, and scenario planning tools to forecast market demand, anticipate industry changes, and capitalize on emerging opportunities that drive business innovation,

resilience, and sustainable growth in the transportation sector.

2. **Performance Metrics and Benchmarking:** Benchmark business performance metrics, financial ratios, and operational benchmarks against industry standards, peer group comparisons, and best-in-class practices to assess performance gaps, identify improvement opportunities, and implement performance improvement strategies that enhance business competitiveness and operational effectiveness. Utilize benchmarking data, industry benchmarks, and performance scorecards to measure progress, track performance trends, and achieve operational excellence in delivering superior transportation services, optimizing resource allocation, and achieving financial sustainability in a competitive marketplace.

3. **Risk Assessment and Mitigation Strategies:** Conduct risk assessments, scenario analysis, and predictive modeling techniques to evaluate business risks, assess potential impacts, and develop risk mitigation strategies that minimize operational disruptions, financial losses, and regulatory compliance risks within your cargo van and box truck business operations. Utilize risk management frameworks, contingency planning, and crisis response protocols to anticipate risks, implement preventive controls, and enhance organizational resilience against emerging threats, cybersecurity risks, and operational vulnerabilities that

may impact business continuity, client relationships, and stakeholder trust in your transportation services.

Implementing Continuous Improvement Strategies

1. **Process Optimization and Workflow Enhancements:** Implement continuous improvement strategies, process optimization initiatives, and workflow enhancements to streamline business operations, reduce operational inefficiencies, and enhance productivity across your cargo van and box truck fleet. Utilize lean management principles, quality improvement methodologies, and performance metrics to identify process bottlenecks, eliminate waste, and optimize workflow processes that drive operational efficiency, cost savings, and service delivery excellence in meeting customer expectations and industry standards.
2. **Employee Training and Development:** Invest in employee training programs, skills development initiatives, and continuous learning opportunities to empower workforce capabilities, enhance job performance, and foster a culture of innovation, collaboration, and continuous improvement within your transportation organization. Provide ongoing training on industry best practices, technological advancements, and safety protocols to equip employees with the knowledge, skills, and

competencies needed to deliver high-quality transportation services, uphold regulatory compliance, and promote operational excellence in driving customer satisfaction, employee engagement, and organizational success in the competitive transportation marketplace.

3. **Feedback Mechanisms and Performance Evaluation:** Establish feedback mechanisms, performance evaluation processes, and stakeholder engagement strategies to solicit input, gather insights, and assess stakeholder satisfaction with your cargo van and box truck business operations. Utilize customer surveys, employee feedback sessions, and supplier evaluations to gather feedback, measure performance outcomes, and identify areas for improvement that enhance service quality, operational efficiency, and stakeholder relationships within your transportation ecosystem. Implement feedback-driven improvements, service enhancements, and continuous monitoring initiatives to address stakeholder expectations, exceed service standards, and drive sustainable growth, profitability, and competitive advantage in delivering value-added transportation solutions to clients, stakeholders, and industry partners.

Conclusion

Leveraging data and analytics is instrumental in optimizing business performance, enhancing decision-making processes, and driving continuous improvement initiatives that promote operational excellence, customer satisfaction, and sustainable growth in your cargo van and box truck business. By tracking and analyzing business performance metrics, utilizing data-driven insights to inform strategic decisions, and implementing continuous improvement strategies, you can achieve operational efficiency, mitigate business risks, and capitalize on growth opportunities that position your transportation business for success in a dynamic and competitive marketplace.

Embrace data-driven innovation, leverage advanced analytics tools, and foster a culture of continuous improvement, collaboration, and operational excellence to drive business transformation, achieve organizational goals, and deliver exceptional value to customers, stakeholders, and industry partners. With a commitment to data-driven decision-making, performance excellence, and continuous improvement initiatives, your cargo van and box truck business can navigate market uncertainties, capitalize on emerging trends, and sustain long-term success as a leader in the transportation industry through innovation, resilience, and strategic agility.

Chapter 23: Legal and Contractual Considerations

Welcome to Chapter 23 of your journey in establishing and growing your cargo van and box truck business. Navigating the legal and contractual landscape is essential to protecting your business interests, ensuring compliance with regulatory requirements, and fostering trust with clients and partners. In this chapter, we will explore key considerations for drafting and reviewing contracts, understanding your legal obligations, and implementing strategies to safeguard your business in the competitive transportation industry.

Drafting and Reviewing Contracts

1. **Contract Essentials:** When drafting contracts for your cargo van and box truck business, clarity and specificity are paramount. Clearly outline the scope of services, payment terms, delivery schedules, and liability provisions to establish clear expectations and prevent misunderstandings. Include details on service guarantees, insurance coverage, and dispute resolution mechanisms to protect your interests and maintain accountability throughout the contractual relationship. Collaborate with legal advisors or contract specialists to draft comprehensive agreements that reflect industry standards, protect against potential risks, and uphold your business reputation as a reliable transportation service provider.

2. **Contractual Agreements:** Formalize agreements with clients, suppliers, and business partners through written contracts that outline rights, responsibilities, and mutual obligations. Include provisions for service levels, performance metrics, and quality standards to uphold service excellence, customer satisfaction, and operational efficiency in delivering transportation services. Review contracts periodically, update terms as needed, and seek legal advice to ensure compliance with regulatory requirements, mitigate contractual risks, and enforce contractual rights in resolving disputes, protecting intellectual property, and safeguarding business interests within your cargo van and box truck business operations.

3. **Negotiation Strategies:** Engage in contract negotiations with clients, suppliers, or business partners to achieve mutually beneficial terms, address concerns, and reach consensus on contractual terms that support business objectives, minimize risks, and foster long-term partnerships. Prioritize transparency, open communication, and collaborative problem-solving to build trust, resolve conflicts, and negotiate fair terms that align with market standards, regulatory compliance, and industry best practices in the transportation sector. Document agreements, finalize contract terms, and obtain legal review to ensure contractual validity, enforceability, and compliance with legal requirements governing business

transactions and contractual obligations within your cargo van and box truck business operations.

Understanding Your Legal Obligations

1. **Business Registration and Licensing:** Register your cargo van and box truck business with relevant government authorities, obtain business licenses, permits, and operating certifications to legally operate as a transportation service provider. Comply with regulatory requirements, zoning laws, and transportation regulations governing vehicle registration, driver licensing, and operational permits to maintain legal compliance, uphold industry standards, and mitigate legal risks associated with business operations in the transportation industry. Consult legal advisors or regulatory experts to navigate licensing procedures, regulatory compliance, and legal obligations that impact your cargo van and box truck business operations in local, regional, or international markets.

2. **Contractual Compliance:** Honor contractual obligations, fulfill service commitments, and adhere to contract terms outlined in agreements with clients, suppliers, and business partners to maintain trust, uphold business reputation, and mitigate legal risks associated with breach of contract claims, disputes, or litigation. Implement contract management protocols,

monitor compliance with contractual terms, and document performance milestones to demonstrate adherence to legal obligations, fulfill service expectations, and resolve contractual disputes through mediation, arbitration, or legal remedies available under contract law.

3. **Risk Management and Liability Protection:** Identify potential risks, assess liability exposures, and implement risk management strategies to protect your cargo van and box truck business against financial losses, legal claims, and operational disruptions arising from accidents, property damage, or third-party liabilities. Secure comprehensive insurance coverage, including commercial liability insurance, vehicle insurance, and cargo insurance to mitigate risks, safeguard business assets, and protect against legal liabilities associated with transportation operations, driver accidents, or property damage incidents within your business operations. Consult insurance brokers or risk management advisors to tailor insurance coverage, assess coverage limits, and mitigate financial risks associated with operational hazards, regulatory compliance, and legal liabilities impacting your cargo van and box truck business operations.

1. **Intellectual Property Protection:** Safeguard intellectual property rights, proprietary information, and business assets through trademark registration, copyright protection, and confidentiality agreements to prevent unauthorized use, infringement, or misappropriation of intellectual property assets within your cargo van and box truck business operations. Implement data security measures, encryption protocols, and access controls to protect sensitive information, customer data, and proprietary technologies from cybersecurity threats, data breaches, or unauthorized access that may compromise business confidentiality, integrity, and trustworthiness in safeguarding intellectual property rights and confidential business information.

2. **Compliance with Regulatory Standards:** Monitor regulatory changes, updates to transportation laws, and industry regulations governing cargo van and box truck operations to ensure compliance with safety standards, environmental regulations, and regulatory requirements that impact business operations. Maintain accurate records, perform safety inspections, and conduct driver training programs to uphold regulatory compliance, mitigate legal risks, and demonstrate due diligence in maintaining operational

safety, vehicle maintenance, and driver qualifications within your transportation business operations.
3. **Legal Counsel and Advisory Support:** Seek legal counsel, advisory support, or professional guidance from legal experts, industry associations, or regulatory authorities to address complex legal issues, interpret regulatory requirements, and navigate legal challenges impacting your cargo van and box truck business operations. Consult legal advisors for legal opinions, regulatory compliance assessments, and legal representation in negotiating contracts, resolving disputes, or defending legal claims that may arise from business transactions, contractual obligations, or regulatory compliance issues within the transportation industry.

Conclusion

Legal and contractual considerations are foundational to the success, integrity, and sustainability of your cargo van and box truck business in the competitive transportation marketplace. By drafting clear contracts, understanding legal obligations, and implementing strategies to protect business interests, you can mitigate legal risks, ensure regulatory compliance, and foster trust with clients, suppliers, and stakeholders. Embrace legal compliance as a strategic priority, invest in legal counsel, and uphold ethical business practices that uphold industry standards, uphold contractual obligations, and safeguard business reputation in delivering reliable transportation services, maintaining customer trust, and achieving long-term success in the dynamic transportation industry landscape.

Chapter 24: Handling Logistics and Distribution

Welcome to Chapter 24 of your journey in managing your cargo van and box truck business. Effectively handling logistics and distribution is crucial for ensuring seamless operations, meeting client expectations, and optimizing delivery efficiency in the competitive transportation industry. In this chapter, we will explore strategies for planning and managing routes, coordinating with clients and suppliers, and ensuring timely deliveries to enhance service reliability, customer satisfaction, and operational effectiveness within your transportation business.

Planning and Managing Routes

1. **Route Optimization Strategies:** Develop route optimization strategies using GPS technology, route planning software, and real-time traffic updates to maximize delivery efficiency, minimize travel time, and reduce fuel consumption across your cargo van and box truck fleet. Analyze geographic data, customer locations, and delivery schedules to create optimized routes that streamline workflow processes, enhance productivity, and optimize resource utilization in

delivering transportation services. Implement routing algorithms, multi-stop route planning, and driver instructions to guide route execution, monitor route performance, and adapt to unforeseen changes or customer requests to maintain service reliability and meet delivery commitments.

2. **Delivery Scheduling and Coordination:** Coordinate delivery schedules, customer orders, and supplier pickups through centralized scheduling systems, dispatch management tools, and communication channels to streamline logistics operations, optimize vehicle utilization, and ensure on-time deliveries within your cargo van and box truck business. Communicate delivery schedules, update order status, and coordinate route changes with clients, suppliers, and internal stakeholders to enhance operational transparency, customer service levels, and responsiveness in managing logistics workflows, order fulfillment, and delivery logistics.

3. **Traffic Management and Real-Time Updates:** Monitor traffic conditions, weather forecasts, and road closures using real-time traffic updates, navigation apps, and GPS tracking systems to optimize route planning, adjust delivery schedules, and mitigate delays that impact delivery times within your cargo van and box truck operations. Utilize alternative routes, traffic rerouting capabilities, and driver communications to navigate traffic congestion, road hazards, and

unforeseen obstacles to maintain delivery timelines, uphold service commitments, and ensure customer satisfaction with reliable transportation services.

Coordinating with Clients and Suppliers

1. **Client Relationship Management:** Foster client relationships, communicate service offerings, and collaborate with clients on delivery schedules, service expectations, and order fulfillment requirements to deliver personalized transportation solutions, exceed customer expectations, and build long-term client loyalty within your cargo van and box truck business. Establish communication channels, customer feedback mechanisms, and client engagement strategies to address client inquiries, resolve service issues, and enhance customer satisfaction with timely, reliable delivery services that align with client needs, preferences, and operational requirements in the transportation industry.
2. **Supplier Collaboration and Partnerships:** Collaborate with suppliers, vendors, and logistics partners to coordinate product pickups, supply chain logistics, and inventory management processes that support seamless operations, supply chain efficiency, and on-time deliveries within your cargo van and box truck business. Establish supplier relationships, negotiate service agreements, and implement supply chain

management practices to optimize inventory replenishment, manage supplier relationships, and support operational logistics that enhance service reliability, reduce lead times, and meet customer demand for transportation services.

3. **Service Coordination and Delivery Fulfillment:** Coordinate service requests, delivery orders, and logistical requirements with internal teams, field personnel, and operational staff to facilitate efficient delivery fulfillment, streamline logistics operations, and ensure timely service delivery within your cargo van and box truck business. Utilize dispatch management systems, order tracking tools, and communication platforms to allocate resources, monitor service requests, and manage delivery schedules that optimize operational efficiency, enhance service responsiveness, and meet customer expectations with reliable transportation solutions that drive business growth and competitive advantage in the transportation industry.

Ensuring Timely Deliveries

1. **Operational Efficiency and Performance Metrics:** Monitor operational performance metrics, delivery performance indicators, and service level agreements (SLAs) to assess delivery performance, track on-time delivery rates, and measure service reliability within

your cargo van and box truck business operations. Utilize performance dashboards, delivery tracking systems, and customer feedback to evaluate delivery efficiency, identify performance gaps, and implement continuous improvement initiatives that optimize delivery processes, enhance service quality, and exceed customer expectations with reliable transportation services that support business growth and operational excellence in the competitive transportation industry.

2. **Customer Service Excellence:** Deliver exceptional customer service, proactive communication, and personalized delivery experiences that meet customer expectations, build trust, and enhance brand reputation within your cargo van and box truck business. Implement customer service protocols, delivery notifications, and service updates to keep customers informed, address delivery inquiries, and resolve service issues promptly to ensure customer satisfaction, loyalty, and retention with reliable transportation solutions that deliver value, reliability, and peace of mind in meeting customer needs, preferences, and operational requirements.

3. **Performance Monitoring and Continuous Improvement:** Monitor delivery performance, analyze delivery metrics, and conduct performance reviews to identify operational inefficiencies, optimize delivery routes, and implement performance improvement

strategies that enhance delivery reliability, reduce delivery times, and improve service outcomes within your cargo van and box truck business operations. Utilize data analytics, performance benchmarking, and operational insights to measure delivery effectiveness, track service performance, and implement continuous improvement initiatives that optimize delivery logistics, enhance operational efficiency, and drive business success in delivering transportation services that exceed customer expectations and support sustainable growth in the transportation industry.

Conclusion

Handling logistics and distribution is integral to the success, efficiency, and customer satisfaction of your cargo van and box truck business. By planning and managing routes effectively, coordinating with clients and suppliers, and ensuring timely deliveries, you can optimize operational efficiency, enhance service reliability, and drive business growth in the competitive transportation marketplace. Embrace logistics management as a strategic imperative, invest in technology solutions, and foster collaborative partnerships that streamline operations, improve delivery performance, and exceed customer expectations with reliable transportation services that deliver value, reliability, and operational excellence in meeting client needs, operational requirements, and market demands in the dynamic and evolving transportation industry landscape.

Chapter 25: Offering Specialty Services

Welcome to Chapter 25 of your journey in expanding and enhancing your cargo van and box truck business. Offering specialty services allows you to explore niche markets, provide specialized transportation solutions, and customize services to meet the unique needs and preferences of clients within the transportation industry. In this chapter, we will explore strategies for identifying niche markets, delivering specialized transportation services, and tailoring service offerings to create value, differentiate your business, and meet diverse client demands in the competitive transportation marketplace.

Exploring Niche Markets

1. **Market Research and Analysis:** Conduct market research to identify emerging trends, market segments, and niche opportunities within the transportation industry that align with your business capabilities, resources, and strategic objectives. Analyze customer demographics, industry dynamics, and market demand for specialized transportation services such as fragile goods transport, temperature-sensitive logistics, last-mile delivery solutions, or specialty freight services that cater to specific client

needs, operational requirements, and market preferences within targeted niche markets.

2. **Client Segmentation:** Segment clients based on industry sectors, geographic locations, and service requirements to prioritize niche markets, tailor service offerings, and customize transportation solutions that address unique client challenges, logistical complexities, and specialized service expectations within your cargo van and box truck business. Develop client profiles, customer personas, and segmentation strategies to identify niche market opportunities, align service offerings, and differentiate your business in delivering value-added transportation services that meet specialized client needs, exceed service expectations, and drive business growth in targeted market segments.

3. **Competitive Analysis:** Evaluate competitive landscape, industry competitors, and market positioning strategies to identify gaps, differentiation opportunities, and competitive advantages that enable your cargo van and box truck business to stand out in specialized transportation services, niche markets, and client-focused solutions. Differentiate your business by offering unique service propositions, innovative solutions, and value-added services that address unmet client needs, capitalize on market opportunities, and position your business as a preferred provider of specialized transportation

services in competitive market segments within the transportation industry.

Providing Specialized Transportation Services

1. **Service Diversification:** Diversify service offerings to include specialized transportation services, value-added solutions, and customized logistics solutions that cater to specific client requirements, operational challenges, and industry-specific demands within targeted niche markets. Expand service capabilities, invest in specialized equipment, and develop expertise in handling specialized cargo, hazardous materials, or oversized freight that require customized transportation solutions, regulatory compliance, and operational excellence in delivering reliable transportation services that meet client expectations and industry standards.

2. **Customized Solutions:** Customize transportation services, logistical solutions, and delivery strategies to meet client-specific needs, project requirements, and operational constraints within specialized market segments such as healthcare logistics, retail distribution, event logistics, or automotive transport that require tailored transportation solutions, real-time tracking capabilities, and supply chain visibility to optimize service delivery, mitigate risks, and ensure operational efficiency in meeting client expectations

with specialized transportation services that enhance business value, customer satisfaction, and competitive differentiation in the transportation marketplace.

3. **Technology Integration:** Integrate technology solutions, advanced logistics software, and real-time tracking systems to enhance operational visibility, optimize route planning, and monitor delivery performance for specialized transportation services that require precision, reliability, and compliance with industry standards, regulatory requirements, and client expectations. Utilize GPS tracking, route optimization tools, and data analytics to optimize transportation logistics, streamline operations, and deliver superior service quality, operational efficiency, and customer satisfaction in providing specialized transportation solutions that address unique client needs, logistical challenges, and industry-specific requirements within targeted niche markets.

Customizing Services to Meet Client Needs

1. **Client Consultation and Needs Assessment:** Conduct client consultations, needs assessments, and solution discovery sessions to understand client requirements, logistics challenges, and service expectations for customized transportation solutions that meet unique client needs, operational constraints, and industry-specific requirements within targeted niche markets.

Collaborate with clients, develop customized service plans, and tailor transportation solutions to address specific project requirements, logistical complexities, and operational objectives that enhance service reliability, optimize resource utilization, and exceed client expectations in delivering specialized transportation services that drive business growth, customer satisfaction, and competitive advantage in the transportation industry.

2. **Service Flexibility and Adaptability:** Offer service flexibility, adaptive logistics solutions, and responsive service delivery options that accommodate changing client demands, operational dynamics, and market fluctuations within specialized transportation services, niche markets, and client-focused solutions. Maintain agility, responsiveness, and operational readiness to adapt to client preferences, adjust service offerings, and optimize service delivery strategies that align with evolving client needs, industry trends, and market demands in delivering customized transportation solutions that enhance service value, operational efficiency, and customer satisfaction within your cargo van and box truck business.

3. **Continuous Improvement and Innovation:** Embrace continuous improvement initiatives, innovation strategies, and service innovation practices to enhance service quality, operational efficiency, and customer satisfaction in delivering specialized transportation

services that exceed client expectations, drive business growth, and differentiate your cargo van and box truck business in competitive niche markets within the transportation industry. Innovate service offerings, leverage emerging technologies, and adopt industry best practices to optimize service delivery, mitigate operational risks, and sustain competitive advantage in providing customized transportation solutions that deliver value, reliability, and customer-centric service excellence within targeted market segments, client relationships, and industry partnerships.

Conclusion

Offering specialty services allows your cargo van and box truck business to explore niche markets, provide specialized transportation solutions, and customize service offerings to meet diverse client needs, operational requirements, and industry-specific demands within the transportation industry. By identifying niche market opportunities, delivering specialized transportation services, and customizing solutions to meet client expectations, you can differentiate your business, enhance service value, and drive business growth in competitive market segments, client relationships, and industry partnerships that sustain long-term success, operational excellence, and customer satisfaction within your cargo van and box truck business operations. Embrace specialization as a strategic advantage, invest in service differentiation, and prioritize client-centric solutions that optimize service delivery, exceed client expectations, and foster sustainable growth in delivering specialized transportation services that drive business innovation, operational efficiency, and competitive differentiation in the dynamic and evolving transportation industry landscape.

Chapter 26: Case Studies and Success Stories

Welcome to Chapter 26, where we delve into real-life examples of successful businesses in the cargo van and box truck industry. By examining these case studies and learning from industry leaders, you'll gain valuable insights, inspiration, and practical strategies to apply to your own business journey. Let's explore how these businesses have achieved success, the lessons they've learned, and how you can adapt their strategies to enhance your own cargo van and box truck business.

Real-Life Examples of Successful Businesses

1. **Example 1: XYZ Transportation Solutions**

    XYZ Transportation Solutions began as a small, local cargo van service catering to businesses in urban areas. Through strategic expansion and a focus on customer service, they diversified their service offerings to include last-mile delivery solutions for e-commerce giants. By investing in technology for route optimization and real-time tracking, XYZ Transportation Solutions optimized their operations, reduced delivery times, and enhanced customer satisfaction. They leveraged partnerships with local businesses and e-commerce platforms to scale their operations while maintaining service excellence and reliability.

2. **Example 2: ABC Logistics**

    ABC Logistics started as a family-owned box truck business specializing in regional freight transport. Recognizing the growing demand for specialized logistics solutions, ABC Logistics expanded their fleet and service capabilities to include temperature-sensitive transport for pharmaceutical companies. By adhering to strict regulatory compliance, investing in specialized equipment, and offering personalized customer service, ABC Logistics established themselves as a trusted partner in the healthcare logistics sector. Their commitment to reliability, safety, and customer satisfaction enabled them to secure long-term contracts and expand their market presence across multiple states.

Lessons Learned from Industry Leaders

1. **Focus on Customer Service:** Successful businesses in the cargo van and box truck industry prioritize

customer service excellence. They understand that timely deliveries, clear communication, and proactive problem-solving are essential for maintaining client trust and loyalty. By consistently exceeding customer expectations, these businesses build strong relationships that lead to repeat business and referrals.

2. **Adaptability and Innovation:** Industry leaders continuously innovate and adapt to changing market dynamics and technological advancements. They embrace new technologies for route optimization, fleet management, and customer communication to improve operational efficiency and service quality. By staying ahead of industry trends and customer preferences, these businesses position themselves as market leaders and innovators in the transportation sector.

3. **Strategic Partnerships:** Collaborations with suppliers, industry associations, and strategic partners play a crucial role in the success of cargo van and box truck businesses. Successful companies forge partnerships that enhance service offerings, expand market reach, and drive business growth. These partnerships enable access to new markets, resources, and expertise that contribute to sustainable business development and competitive advantage in the transportation industry.

1. **Embrace Continuous Learning:** Learn from the experiences and successes of industry leaders to refine your business strategies, enhance operational efficiency, and achieve sustainable growth. Adopt a growth mindset, seek opportunities for professional development, and stay informed about industry trends, regulatory changes, and technological innovations that impact your cargo van and box truck business.
2. **Focus on Quality and Reliability:** Prioritize service quality, reliability, and operational excellence in delivering transportation solutions that meet client expectations and exceed industry standards. Invest in training programs, quality assurance measures, and customer feedback mechanisms to continuously improve service delivery, mitigate operational risks, and enhance customer satisfaction within your cargo van and box truck business operations.
3. **Build a Strong Company Culture:** Cultivate a positive work environment, foster teamwork, and empower employees to contribute to business success and customer satisfaction. Invest in employee training, professional development opportunities, and recognition programs to promote employee engagement, morale, and retention within your cargo van and box truck business. By building a strong

company culture based on integrity, collaboration, and accountability, you create a supportive workplace environment that attracts talent, drives performance, and promotes organizational success in the transportation industry.

Conclusion

Case studies and success stories from industry leaders provide valuable insights, inspiration, and practical strategies for enhancing your cargo van and box truck business. By learning from real-life examples of successful businesses, embracing lessons learned from industry leaders, and gaining inspiration and insights for your business journey, you can apply proven strategies, adopt innovative approaches, and differentiate your business in the competitive transportation marketplace. Embrace continuous learning, focus on customer service excellence, and build strategic partnerships that drive business growth, operational efficiency, and customer satisfaction within your cargo van and box truck business operations. By leveraging inspiration and insights from industry leaders, you can navigate challenges, capitalize on opportunities, and achieve sustainable success in delivering transportation solutions that meet client needs, exceed industry standards, and drive business innovation in the dynamic and evolving transportation industry landscape.

Chapter 27: Common Challenges and How to Overcome Them

Welcome to Chapter 27, where we explore the common challenges faced by cargo van and box truck businesses and strategies to overcome them. Understanding these obstacles and learning from failures can empower you to navigate challenges effectively, build resilience, and achieve sustainable success in the competitive transportation industry. Let's delve into the typical challenges encountered, practical strategies for overcoming them, and valuable lessons learned along the way.

Identifying Typical Obstacles

1. **Fuel Costs and Operating Expenses:** Rising fuel costs, maintenance expenses, and operational overheads pose significant financial challenges for cargo van and box truck businesses. Fluctuating fuel prices and unexpected maintenance issues can strain profitability and impact operational efficiency. Managing operating expenses, optimizing fuel efficiency, and implementing preventive maintenance schedules are essential strategies to mitigate financial pressures and maintain cost-effective operations in the transportation industry.
2. **Regulatory Compliance and Safety:** Navigating complex regulatory requirements, compliance with transportation laws, and ensuring vehicle safety

standards present regulatory challenges for cargo van and box truck businesses. Failure to adhere to regulations can result in fines, penalties, and disruptions to business operations. Establishing robust compliance programs, conducting regular safety inspections, and providing ongoing driver training are critical measures to ensure regulatory adherence, enhance safety protocols, and mitigate legal risks within your transportation operations.

3. **Driver Shortages and Workforce Management:** Recruiting qualified drivers, addressing driver shortages, and managing workforce dynamics are common staffing challenges in the transportation industry. High turnover rates, driver retention issues, and labor shortages can impact service reliability and operational continuity. Implementing competitive compensation packages, driver retention strategies, and workforce development programs can attract talent, improve driver retention rates, and foster a skilled workforce capable of delivering exceptional service in your cargo van and box truck business.

Strategies for Overcoming Challenges

1. **Financial Management and Cost Control:** Develop comprehensive financial management strategies, monitor budgetary expenditures, and implement cost-control measures to manage fuel costs, operational

expenses, and overheads effectively. Utilize financial forecasting tools, negotiate vendor contracts, and optimize route planning to reduce operational costs, improve profit margins, and maintain financial stability within your cargo van and box truck business.

2. **Technology Adoption and Innovation:** Embrace technology solutions, fleet management software, and real-time tracking systems to enhance operational visibility, optimize route planning, and improve fleet efficiency in your cargo van and box truck business. Invest in GPS tracking, telematics devices, and fleet analytics tools to monitor vehicle performance, optimize fuel usage, and streamline logistics operations that enhance service reliability, operational efficiency, and customer satisfaction in the transportation industry.

3. **Risk Management and Contingency Planning:** Develop risk management strategies, assess operational risks, and implement contingency plans to mitigate unforeseen challenges, disruptions, and emergencies that impact service delivery in your cargo van and box truck business. Maintain emergency response protocols, establish business continuity plans, and conduct scenario-based training exercises to prepare for adverse situations, minimize downtime, and ensure operational resilience in delivering transportation solutions that meet client expectations and industry standards.

1. **Adaptability and Flexibility:** Embrace a culture of adaptability, flexibility, and continuous improvement to learn from failures, address operational challenges, and implement corrective actions that drive business resilience and growth in the transportation industry. Analyze failure points, identify root causes, and implement process improvements to enhance operational efficiency, mitigate risks, and optimize service delivery within your cargo van and box truck business operations.

2. **Collaboration and Industry Partnerships:** Foster collaborative partnerships, engage industry stakeholders, and leverage supplier relationships to address operational challenges, navigate regulatory complexities, and drive business innovation in the transportation sector. Collaborate with industry associations, regulatory bodies, and strategic partners to share best practices, access industry insights, and implement innovative solutions that enhance operational performance, regulatory compliance, and service excellence in delivering transportation services that exceed client expectations and support sustainable growth in the competitive transportation industry.

Conclusion

Navigating common challenges in the cargo van and box truck business requires proactive strategies, resilience, and continuous learning to overcome obstacles, achieve operational excellence, and sustain business success in the transportation industry. By identifying typical challenges, implementing effective strategies, and learning from failures, you can strengthen operational resilience, enhance service reliability, and drive business growth within your cargo van and box truck business operations. Embrace innovation, prioritize regulatory compliance, and foster a culture of continuous improvement to navigate challenges, seize opportunities, and achieve sustainable success in delivering transportation solutions that meet client needs, exceed industry standards, and drive business innovation in the dynamic and evolving transportation industry landscape.

Chapter 28: Future Trends in the Cargo Van and Box Truck Industry

Welcome to Chapter 28, where we explore the exciting future trends shaping the cargo van and box truck industry. As technology advances and consumer demands evolve, staying ahead of emerging trends and innovations is crucial for preparing your business to thrive in the dynamic transportation landscape. Let's delve into the key trends, industry forecasts, and strategies to future-proof your cargo van and box truck business for success.

Emerging Technologies and Innovations

1. **Electric and Alternative Fuel Vehicles:** The shift towards sustainability and environmental responsibility is driving the adoption of electric and alternative fuel vehicles in the transportation industry. Electric cargo vans and box trucks offer reduced carbon emissions, lower operating costs, and compliance with stringent environmental regulations. As battery technology advances and charging infrastructure expands, businesses are increasingly integrating electric vehicles into their fleets to achieve operational efficiency, environmental sustainability, and cost savings in delivering transportation solutions.
2. **Autonomous Vehicles and Robotics:** Autonomous technology and robotics are revolutionizing last-mile delivery and logistics operations in the cargo van and

box truck industry. Automated vehicles, drones, and robotic systems enable efficient route planning, contactless deliveries, and enhanced operational productivity. As autonomous technology matures and regulatory frameworks evolve, businesses are exploring autonomous delivery solutions to optimize logistics, improve delivery speed, and meet growing consumer expectations for fast and reliable transportation services.

3. **Data Analytics and Predictive Insights:** Big data analytics, AI-driven algorithms, and predictive analytics are transforming decision-making processes and operational efficiency in the transportation sector. Real-time data analytics enable businesses to optimize route planning, predict demand patterns, and enhance fleet management strategies. By harnessing data-driven insights, cargo van and box truck businesses can improve resource allocation, reduce operational costs, and deliver personalized transportation solutions that align with client preferences and market dynamics.

Industry Forecasts and Predictions

1. **E-commerce Growth and Last-Mile Delivery:** The rapid growth of e-commerce and online retail continues to drive demand for efficient last-mile delivery solutions in the cargo van and box truck industry. Industry forecasts predict continued expansion of e-commerce

sales, leading to increased demand for same-day and next-day delivery services. Businesses are investing in advanced logistics technologies, urban distribution centers, and micro-fulfillment strategies to enhance delivery speed, optimize inventory management, and meet consumer expectations for fast, reliable, and convenient transportation services.

2. **Urbanization and Mobility Solutions:** Urbanization trends and population growth in metropolitan areas are reshaping transportation logistics and mobility solutions in the cargo van and box truck industry. Cities are implementing smart city initiatives, congestion pricing policies, and sustainable urban mobility plans to reduce traffic congestion, improve air quality, and enhance transportation efficiency. Businesses are adapting by investing in electric vehicles, micro-mobility solutions, and urban logistics strategies to navigate urban environments, optimize delivery routes, and support sustainable urban development goals.

3. **Customer Experience and Personalization:** Consumer preferences for personalized experiences and seamless delivery services are driving innovation in the cargo van and box truck industry. Businesses are investing in customer relationship management (CRM) systems, mobile applications, and delivery tracking platforms to enhance transparency, communication, and real-time updates throughout the delivery process. By

prioritizing customer experience, personalization, and service reliability, businesses can differentiate their brands, build customer loyalty, and gain a competitive edge in the increasingly competitive transportation marketplace.

Preparing Your Business for the Future

1. **Investment in Technology and Innovation:** Stay ahead of industry trends by investing in cutting-edge technologies, fleet management software, and logistics innovations that enhance operational efficiency, optimize resource utilization, and improve service delivery in your cargo van and box truck business. Embrace digital transformation, adopt cloud-based solutions, and integrate IoT devices to streamline operations, automate workflows, and leverage data-driven insights for informed decision-making in delivering transportation solutions that meet future market demands and client expectations.
2. **Adaptability and Flexibility:** Embrace a culture of adaptability, flexibility, and continuous learning to navigate evolving market trends, regulatory changes, and technological advancements in the cargo van and box truck industry. Anticipate future challenges, proactively adjust business strategies, and capitalize on emerging opportunities to maintain competitive advantage, drive business growth, and achieve long-

term success in delivering transportation services that align with client needs, industry standards, and market dynamics.

3. **Strategic Partnerships and Collaboration:** Foster collaborative partnerships, engage with industry stakeholders, and leverage strategic alliances to access new markets, expand service capabilities, and drive innovation in your cargo van and box truck business. Collaborate with technology providers, logistics experts, and regulatory authorities to navigate industry complexities, implement best practices, and pioneer sustainable solutions that enhance operational efficiency, regulatory compliance, and service excellence in delivering transportation services that anticipate future trends, exceed client expectations, and support business growth in the dynamic and evolving cargo van and box truck industry landscape.

Conclusion

Embracing future trends, emerging technologies, and industry forecasts positions your cargo van and box truck business for success in the dynamic transportation industry. By harnessing the power of electric vehicles, autonomous technology, data analytics, and customer-centric innovations, you can optimize operational efficiency, enhance service reliability, and drive business growth in delivering transportation solutions that meet evolving market demands, exceed client expectations, and support sustainable development goals in the competitive landscape of the future. Prepare your business for the future by investing in technology, fostering innovation, and cultivating strategic partnerships that enable you to navigate challenges, capitalize on opportunities, and achieve sustainable success in delivering transportation services that drive business innovation, operational excellence, and customer satisfaction in the dynamic and evolving cargo van and box truck industry landscape.

Chapter 29: Building a Legacy

Welcome to Chapter 29, where we explore the importance of building a legacy in your cargo van and box truck business. Building a legacy goes beyond short-term success; it involves creating a long-term vision, planning for succession, and leaving a lasting impact that extends beyond your own involvement in the business. Let's delve into how you can shape a legacy that reflects your values, contributes to industry advancement, and ensures the continuity of your business for future generations.

Creating a Long-Term Vision for Your Business

1. **Define Your Core Values and Mission:** Building a legacy begins with defining your business's core values, mission, and long-term objectives. Identify what sets your cargo van and box truck business apart, articulate

your commitment to service excellence, safety standards, and customer satisfaction. Establish a clear vision that aligns with your personal values and reflects the legacy you aspire to leave in the transportation industry.

2. **Strategic Planning and Goal Setting:** Develop a strategic plan that outlines actionable goals, milestones, and growth strategies for your cargo van and box truck business. Set measurable objectives for fleet expansion, market expansion, and revenue growth while maintaining a focus on sustainability, operational efficiency, and service innovation. Align your long-term vision with strategic planning initiatives that position your business for sustainable growth, industry leadership, and long-term success in delivering transportation solutions that exceed client expectations and support business continuity for future generations.

Succession Planning

1. **Identify Succession Candidates:** Succession planning involves identifying potential successors within your organization or family who possess the leadership qualities, industry expertise, and commitment to carry forward your legacy in the cargo van and box truck business. Evaluate key employees, family members, or external candidates who demonstrate potential to lead

the business effectively and uphold its values, vision, and operational standards.

2. **Develop Leadership and Mentorship Programs:** Foster leadership development and mentorship programs to groom successors, impart industry knowledge, and cultivate managerial skills necessary for future leadership roles within your cargo van and box truck business. Provide mentorship, professional development opportunities, and hands-on training experiences that empower successors to make informed decisions, drive strategic initiatives, and uphold the legacy of excellence established in delivering transportation solutions that meet client needs, exceed industry standards, and support sustainable growth in the competitive transportation marketplace.

Leaving a Lasting Impact

1. **Community Engagement and Corporate Social Responsibility:** Build a legacy of corporate social responsibility by engaging with local communities, supporting charitable initiatives, and promoting environmental stewardship within your cargo van and box truck business operations. Implement sustainable business practices, reduce carbon footprint, and contribute to community development projects that enhance quality of life, promote social equity, and

create positive impact beyond business operations. Leave a lasting legacy of corporate citizenship, ethical leadership, and community service that reflects your commitment to making a difference in the lives of others and contributing to a sustainable future for generations to come.

2. **Industry Leadership and Innovation:** Establish your cargo van and box truck business as a leader in the transportation industry by embracing innovation, adopting cutting-edge technologies, and driving industry advancements that enhance operational efficiency, service reliability, and customer satisfaction. Pioneer new solutions, collaborate with industry stakeholders, and advocate for regulatory reforms that promote industry growth, sustainability, and economic prosperity. Leave a legacy of innovation, thought leadership, and industry excellence that inspires future generations to innovate, challenge the status quo, and drive positive change in the dynamic and evolving transportation industry landscape.

Conclusion

Building a legacy in your cargo van and box truck business requires vision, strategic planning, and a commitment to leaving a lasting impact that extends beyond financial success. By creating a long-term vision that aligns with your core values, planning for succession, and embracing corporate social responsibility, you can shape a legacy of excellence, ethical leadership, and industry innovation that withstands the test of time. Prepare your business for future success, empower future leaders, and leave a legacy that inspires, empowers, and contributes to a sustainable future for generations to come in the competitive and evolving landscape of the cargo van and box truck industry

Chapter 30: Conclusion and Next Steps

Congratulations on reaching the conclusion of this journey through the intricacies of starting and running a successful cargo van and box truck business. Throughout this guide, we've explored every aspect from industry insights and operational strategies to future trends and building a lasting legacy. As you prepare to embark on your entrepreneurial journey or further develop your existing business, let's recap the key points, outline actionable steps to get started, and offer encouragement and final thoughts to inspire your next steps.

Recap of Key Points

1. **Industry Overview and Opportunities:** The cargo van and box truck industry offer diverse opportunities driven by e-commerce growth, urbanization, and evolving consumer expectations for fast and reliable delivery services.

2. **Business Planning and Strategic Development:** Developing a robust business plan, setting clear goals, and implementing strategic initiatives are crucial for laying a solid foundation and achieving long-term success in the competitive transportation industry.
3. **Legal and Regulatory Compliance:** Understanding and complying with business registration, licensing requirements, insurance obligations, and transportation regulations are essential to ensure legal compliance and operational integrity.
4. **Fleet Management and Technology Integration:** Choosing the right vehicles, adopting technology solutions such as GPS tracking and fleet management software, and implementing efficient logistics strategies optimize fleet performance and enhance service delivery.
5. **Customer Service Excellence:** Providing exceptional customer service, handling feedback, and building long-term relationships are fundamental to maintaining customer satisfaction, retention, and business growth.
6. **Future Trends and Innovation:** Embracing emerging technologies, sustainability practices, and industry trends positions your business to adapt, innovate, and thrive in a rapidly evolving market environment.

Actionable Steps to Get Started

1. **Evaluate Your Business Plan:** Review and refine your business plan based on insights gained from this guide. Ensure it aligns with your long-term vision, goals, and market opportunities.
2. **Implement Legal and Regulatory Requirements:** Take necessary steps to register your business, obtain required licenses and insurance, and ensure compliance with transportation regulations in your jurisdiction.
3. **Invest in Fleet and Technology:** Select appropriate vehicles, invest in fleet management tools, and integrate technology solutions to streamline operations, enhance efficiency, and improve service delivery.
4. **Focus on Customer Experience:** Develop customer service strategies, implement feedback mechanisms, and prioritize customer satisfaction to build a loyal customer base and differentiate your business in the marketplace.
5. **Monitor Industry Trends:** Stay informed about industry trends, technological advancements, and market dynamics. Continuously adapt your strategies to capitalize on opportunities and mitigate challenges.
6. **Plan for Growth and Sustainability:** Develop growth strategies, explore new service offerings or markets,

and incorporate sustainable practices to foster business expansion and long-term sustainability.

Encouragement and Final Thoughts

As you embark on this entrepreneurial journey or continue to grow your cargo van and box truck business, remember that challenges will arise, but each challenge presents an opportunity for growth and innovation. Stay adaptable, embrace change, and leverage your passion for delivering exceptional service to customers. Seek mentorship, network with industry peers, and never stop learning.

Your commitment to excellence, dedication to customer satisfaction, and strategic foresight will be key drivers of your success. Celebrate milestones, learn from setbacks, and stay focused on your long-term goals. Building a business is a journey filled with ups and downs, but with perseverance, resilience, and a clear vision, you have the potential to create a thriving business that leaves a lasting legacy in the cargo van and box truck industry.

Remember, success is not just measured by financial achievements but also by the positive impact you make on customers, employees, and the community. Your journey towards building and growing a successful cargo van and box truck business starts now. Embrace the challenges, seize the opportunities, and enjoy the fulfillment of building something meaningful and enduring.

Best wishes on your entrepreneurial endeavors and may your journey be filled with growth, prosperity, and fulfillment as you navigate the dynamic and rewarding world of the cargo van and box truck industry!

Conclusion

Dear Reader,

Congratulations on completing this comprehensive guide on starting and running a successful cargo van and box truck business. Throughout these chapters, we've explored every facet of the industry, from initial planning and legal considerations to fleet management, customer service excellence, and future trends. It's been a journey of discovery, learning, and preparation for the exciting road ahead.

As you embark on your entrepreneurial journey or continue to grow your existing business, I wish you nothing but the utmost success. May your business thrive with each mile driven, each satisfied customer served, and each new challenge overcome. Remember, every obstacle is an opportunity in disguise, and every success is a testament to your dedication and perseverance.

Stay true to your vision, uphold your commitment to excellence, and embrace innovation in all that you do. Whether you're just starting out or expanding your operations, may your passion for delivering outstanding service propel you forward. Your journey is not just about building a business—it's about leaving a lasting legacy in the industry, making a positive impact on your community, and creating opportunities for future generations.

Thank you for choosing this guide as your companion on this entrepreneurial path. I trust it has equipped you with the knowledge, insights, and inspiration needed to navigate the challenges and capitalize on the opportunities that lie ahead. Here's to your success, your growth, and your unwavering determination to build something extraordinary in the dynamic world of cargo van and box truck businesses.

www.ingramcontent.com/pod-product-compliance
Lightning Source LLC
Chambersburg PA
CBHW071921210526
45479CB00002B/504